Ready to Go

Retreats & Lock-Ins

16 Complete Plans for Fun and Soulful Events

Beth Miller

08 09 10 11 12 13 14 15– 10 9 8 7 6 5 4 3

MANUFACTURED IN THE UNITED STATES OF AMERICA

Editorial Team
Editor: Jennifer A. Youngman
Production Editor: Susan Heinemann
Writer: Beth Miller

Design Team
Design Manager: Keely Moore
Designer: Keely Moore
Cover Design: Keitha Vincent

Notes on Video Viewing

When you show home videocassettes or DVDs to a group of learners, you need to obtain a license. You can get a public performance license (sometimes called a site or umbrella license) from Christian Video Licensing International (888-302-6020). The license can cost over $100. Check with your church to see if an umbrella license has already been obtained. Many denominations—through conferences, jurisdictions, dioceses, and other structures—secure licenses for their staff to show videos.

Contents

Extended Time 5

Planning Your Retreat 7

Designing Your Retreat Plan 11

Retreats

Seek and Find...17

Learning Love...25

Grace and the Good Shepherd 32

Light Your Soul Fire 43

Faith Prints...56

Soul Mates: Friends for the Journey 67

Hope: the Rock 77

Christmas Retreat...82

Lenten Retreat 87

On the CD-ROM

Lock-ins: Seek and Find; Learning Love; Grace and the Good
Shepherd; Light Your Soul Fire; Faith Prints; Soul
Mates: Friends for the Journey; and Hope: the Rock

Reproducible pages for each retreat

Sample forms: Group Covenant, Registration Form and
Information Sheet, and Transportation Covenant

Dedication

This book could not have been written without the love and participation of the youth and adults of First United Methodist Church of Ann Arbor. Over the past eleven years, we've shared over twenty-five retreats together. These retreats have offered sacred spaces where lives were healed and renewed. I cherish the memories of spirit-filled prayer around campfires; shared silence in the presence of awesome sunrises; polar-bear swims in cold, northern lakes, late-night giggles; the senior girls' midnight raids on the kitchen to get ice cream; and seventh-grade boys begging for more guided-imagery prayer time. Each retreat offered unique, serendipitous experiences.

I'm grateful for the support and love of my family. Megan, as a high school student, field tested much of the material prior to each retreat; if it passed the Megan test, I knew it wasn't too cheesy. Josh was able to serve as a counselor and primary organizer of fun, off-the-wall activities for a couple of retreats. (The legend of the Spam Olympics lives on.) And Nathan, home from college, sat at the evening campfire at my first Ann Arbor retreat and expressed how fortunate the youth were to have his mother as their Youth Director. He thanked me for nurturing him in faith. That initial vote of confidence from my son still means so much. Gilson, my husband, believes in me and encourages me to do more than I ever thought I was capable of. I am blessed!

Joyfully,

Beth Miller

Extended Time

Retreats and Lock-ins

Retreats and lock-ins are effective ways to encourage renewal and reflection. On these trips and overnights, the contact hours with youth are typically more than you might have over the course of several months. Retreats and lock-ins give you and your teens extended time to build relationships with each other and with God.

You can probably think of several compelling reasons to have a retreat or lock-in. But prioritizing your goals will help you offer an event that is gratifying and spiritually significant. Most retreats and lock-ins include fun and fellowship, spiritual growth, community building, rest, reflection, and renewal. Knowing your number-one priority while keeping the other objectives in mind will help focus your planning efforts, pointing you to the right kinds of facilities and programming.

Whatever your main goal, include exercises that draw people together, create a sense of community, and help youth laugh and have fun. But remember that teens also want spiritual growth. They take an interest in activities that give significant insight into faith and that deepen their spiritual growth. Fun and faith are not antithetical.

Retreats Versus *Lock-ins*

Although this book includes both retreats and lock-ins, I want to challenge the common model of youth lock-ins. Typically these events enforce a no-sleep policy and have scheduled activities for every minute of twelve hours. Because recent brain research argues against keeping young people up all night (which I can't do anymore, anyway), I have included some lock-ins with time for both sleep and play, eating, fellowship, and worship.

These mini-retreats are twelve hour versions of the full weekend retreats. As with retreats that have small-group activities, pre-assign small groups for lock-ins with such activities. (See page 9.)

Most youth groups have lock-ins; youth are always asking for them. The lock-ins (on CD-ROM) are the best way to hold them. Make them twelve-hour sabbath times for your group. I can almost guarantee that they will appreciate the opportunity to hang out, relax, and rest.

Planning Your Retreat

CHOOSING A FACILITY

So you've decided to go on retreat. You have dates in mind. One of the first steps is securing a facility. Ideally you will have several camp settings to choose from. Camps often book a year in advance and require a deposit to hold the space, so plan ahead. If you can't get the camp you want, ask to be put on a waiting list in case room becomes available.

Smaller groups have more flexibility and options for lodging. Consider another church, a family cottage or cabin, the woods where you can camp, a university dorm or guesthouse, or a hotel.

PUBLICITY

As soon as dates and a facility are confirmed, publish the dates in the church newsletter, bulletin, e-mail blasts, or website. Schedule the retreat far enough in advance that the youth, parents, and volunteers can set the weekend aside on their calendars. If you announce the dates less than three months before the retreat, a lot of youth will have already made plans for that weekend.

COST

To estimate the cost of the retreat, figure in the following:

→ lodging and meals
→ any meals en route
→ van rentals and gas
→ program expenses

Then find out if you need to include the adult volunteers' lodging and meals in the cost per person or if your church will absorb those costs. Your church's liability policy may cover insurance; your church's budget may provide some funds for the overall retreat or at least provide scholarship money for youth who need it. Think ahead and make arrangements so that money never becomes a deterrent for teen participation.

REGISTRATION FORMS

You always need a parental permission form to take youth offsite. Include on that form the retreat's time, location, and cost; what to bring; what not to bring; and when and how to register. A sample registration is on the CD-ROM. Mail these sheets to every teen on your mailing list. (Retreats can be entry points for youth if you design these trips to be inclusive and welcoming.) If you have a church or youth group website, post a registration form there.

TRANSPORTATION

Often, safety procedures are initiated only after an accident. Be proactive, putting a transportation policy in place and distributing it. On the CD-ROM is a sample transportation covenant for youth and adult leaders.

Once you have a policy, enforce it. Expect your adult leaders to follow the speed limit, and advise them to pull over and refuse to keep driving if seat belts are not fastened or if unruly behavior is distracting them from driving. Most auto-rental insurance policies require drivers to be at least twenty-three years of age, as do most car-rental companies.

Assign the youth to vehicles; doing so will help mix up the group, break up cliques, and create community. In each automobile, put a folder with emergency forms for each passenger. Each van should have a first-aid kit, a garbage bag, tissues, wet wipes, a list of emergency numbers, a list of cell phone numbers of other van drivers and a contact person back home to call if an emergency happens in route and they can't reach another van.

INSURANCE

Verify that the church's insurance policy will cover the retreat. If the policy does not, work out a plan, even if it's just for the retreat weekend.

GROUP NORMS AND EXPECTATIONS

A behavior covenant will help you clarify your expectations and establish consequences for infringement of these guidelines. A sample covenant is on CD-ROM. Require that all retreat participants sign a covenant before the retreat. You might have the youth and the parents sign this form at the start of the school year so that you can use it for all youth group activities.

VAN AND ROOMING PLANS

To build community in your group, establish van and room groups prior to the trip. Do not reveal the assignments until departure, and refuse to change them. (Don't be surprised when parents beg you to move their children to be with their best friends.) Remind the youth that accepting someone translates into the ability to talk to, listen to, and learn more about that person.

Make room assignments, and post them on the outside of each room. (Doing so will help you know if someone is missing from a room and locate someone at night in the case of an emergency.)

SMALL GROUPS

To help build community, designate small groups in advance. Most of this book's retreats include small-group activities. If you have student leaders, assign them leadership roles.

SCHEDULE

Have a schedule, but be flexible, including what you want from the suggested options in this resource. Provide copies of the schedule, and post them in the rooms. For a sample schedule of a retreat, see pages 14–15.

Whichever options you choose, enforce lights out and allow at least eight hours of rest. Research shows that teenagers are the most sleep-deprived group in our culture. The consequences of inadequate sleep include irritability, inability to focus, and an increased vulnerability to illness. These things should not happen on retreats, which are times of spiritual and physical renewal. Teens naturally stay up later and sleep in if given the opportunity. Most teens function better if you allow them to follow these natural inclinations. You can accommodate this tendency by scheduling breakfast as late as possible and scheduling bedtime between eleven and midnight.

INCORPORATING RITUALS AND SURPRISES INTO THE RETREAT

Rituals create memorable experiences that give teens a sense of identity, community, and security. They are also just plain fun. (A word of caution, though: Once you begin a ritual, the youth will remind you that "you always do this on retreat!")

Think about fun photo ops en route: large statues, roadside attractions, and unusual signs. During the retreat, take a cue from hotels and leave a surprise on each pillow before bedtime, such as a mint with a nighttime blessing or Scripture. Draw names for secret prayer pals for the weekend, and reveal these names in a unique way at the closing of the retreat.

SAFETY PROCEDURES FOR LOCK-INS AND RETREATS

No one should leave the retreat site without direct permission from the youth leader. No one should go anywhere alone, so establish a groups-of-three-or-more rule for free time or sightseeing. Expect everyone to follow the schedule and participate in scheduled events. Exceptions for illness and injury should be granted only with the permission of the youth leader.

YOUTH-ADULT-RATIO RECOMMENDATIONS

For on-site youth activities when other adults are present in the building, have one adult for every twenty youth. For on-site youth activities when other adults are not present in the building, have at least two adults.

For off-site youth activities, have one adult per ten youth.

For overnights and weekend retreats, have at least two adults per fifteen youth, including at least one male and one female counselor.

For trips of five nights or more, have one adult (at least one male and one female adult) for every six youth, including at least two drivers for every van.

POLICIES FOR THE SAFETY OF YOUTH

Your church should have a policy statement for the safety and protection of young people. Here is a sample statement:

> (Your church's name here) is a spiritual community that takes seriously our responsibility to provide a safe and nurturing environment for youth who participate in its ministries. All volunteers and employees who have leadership roles in these ministries are living out the vows we take in baptism to nurture our young people in the Christian faith. Everyone plays key roles in fostering the spiritual development of individuals and families in the church community.

Designing Your Retreat Plan

SET THE STAGE WITH PRAYER

At your first gathering as a group, begin with prayer. Pray for God's blessing on your retreat, and thank God for this opportunity. Affirm that God's Spirit has brought each person to live together for this time in Christian community. Remember that where two or three persons gather in God's name, God promises to be present.

ORIENTATION

Welcome everyone, and make nametags. To identify small groups, give each group's nametag a particular color, shape, or sticker. Begin orientation with a group circle and prayer. Introduce your adult leaders and your host, who may be the camp director or site manager. Ask this representative of the facility to go over any policies. Point out emergency phones and first-aid kits, and describe evacuation procedures. Go over behavior expectations.

MAILBOXES

Mailboxes are a fun ritual to include on all retreats. Each person decorates his or her mailbox, and the decorating could take place at a regular youth meeting prior to the retreat. The boxes can be as simple as brown lunch bags decorated with markers. Look for items such as potato-chip cans, VHS cases, manila envelopes, and cereal boxes.

For the decorating of mailboxes, you might provide materials such as stickers, used greeting cards, paper, rubber stamps with ink pads, and magazines. Each student's name should appear clearly on his or her mailbox. Encourage the participants to write affirmations to others and deposit those writings in the mailboxes during the retreat. To assure that everyone gets at least one piece of mail, ask the leaders to write each youth in their small groups; ahead of time give the leaders the names of those in their small groups.

LARGE-GROUP EVENING ACTIVITIES

Large-group evening activities facilitate community building. The focus is on fun, do what would be the most fun for your group. Ideas include a treasure or scavenger hunt, playing a TV-type game such as *Jeopardy!* or *Family Feud,* taking a favorite childhood game (such as hide and seek or capture the flag) and extending the boundaries or adding unusual rules, a funny fashion show, or a talent or no-talent show, and human foosball.

MORNING INDIVIDUAL MEDITATIONS

Included in most of the retreats is a reproducible meditation for each morning. Meet together to pray before beginning this individual meditation time. Remind everyone to be respectful of others and to allow them privacy. Encourage each youth to find a place to be alone and meditate. Provide some signal, such as ringing a bell, to signal when meditation time is over.

GAMES AND RECREATION

Retreats offer space to get away from distractions and build personal interactive skills. So schedule a block of time for group games or insert them throughout the retreat, in between sessions.

For games, you can find websites with excellent, comprehensive resources. Look for games that level the playing field rather than favor the more athletically inclined, as well as noncompetitive games, which avoid winners and losers and provide fun for everyone.

FREE TIME

Free time can mean nap time, study time, or hanging-out time. Consider providing options for free time that will become gathering points for groups of youth. These times will give the teens additional opportunities to become better acquainted while learning a new skill. Ask adult or student leaders to consider what sports, hobbies, or crafts they might contribute to free time.

Here are some ideas: group runs, pick-up-basketball or touch-football games, creating thank-you or birthday cards or cards for college students or people who are homebound, crocheting or knitting, and yoga.

PRAYER STATIONS

Some of the retreats include opportunities for prayer stations. You do not need to use every station, but have enough of them so that only four or five youth will be circulating around them and visiting them one at a time.

At each prayer station, set out a copy of the instructions or meditations (on CD-ROM) for that station. If you don't have enough small tables or benches for all of the stations, use plastic storage bins and cover the bins and tables with material. (Check thrift shops or rummage sales for old sheets, tablecloths, place mats, or bed spreads that you can cut up for coverings.) At each prayer station, use candles and the supplies listed on the CD-ROM's handouts for the stations.

Create a central altar, leaving enough room around it for people to sit. Some retreats include the small groups finding (or making things) to bring to the altar. If your chosen retreat includes this option, use a low table or bench for an altar. Cover it with material, arrange several candles placed on safe surfaces, and include any symbols that reinforce your retreat theme.

YOUTH-DESIGNED CLOSING WORSHIP

Have the students plan and lead a final worship service. Provide time in the schedule for the youth to prepare for this experience. Encourage the teens to be innovative and authentic as they interpret and reflect on the retreat theme.

THEMED RETREATS

The following chapters contain small-group sessions, handouts, activities, and meditations for retreats based on a particular theme.

Dramas that could be added to particular retreats can be found in *Worship Feast: Dramas.*

Additional worship services on some of the themes can be found in *Worship Feast: Services.* This book, along with *Worship Feast: Ideas* and *Worship Feast: Taizé,* provides an excellent resource for creating meaningful worship experiences for your retreat.

SAMPLE SCHEDULES

On the following pages is an idea of what a retreat schedule might look like. Create your own schedule based on your personal style and the activities you choose.

- *Worship Feast: Dramas—15 Sketches for Youth Group, Worship, & More,* by Beth Miller (Abingdon Press, 2003; ISBN 0687044596).

- *Worship Feast: Services—50 Complete Multisensory Services for Youth* (Abingdon Press, 2003; ISBN 0687063671).

- *Worship Feast: Ideas—100 Awesome Ideas for Postmodern Youth* (Abingdon Press, 2004; ISBN 0687063574).

- *Worship Feast: Taizé—20 Complete Services in the Spirit of Taizé* (Abingdon Press, 2004; ISBN 068741912), which includes a split-track CD, and *Worship Feast: Taizé Songbook* (ISBN 0687739322).

SAMPLE SCHEDULE FOR A TWO NIGHT, SPIRITUAL-LIFE RETREAT

Friday

7:00	Arrive at retreat site, settle into rooms
7:30	Group orientation, mailboxes
8:00	Get-acquainted activities
8:45	Snack break
9:00	Meditation time, singing and prayer
10:00	Everyone in his or her room
11:00	Lights out

Saturday

8:00	Breakfast
9:00	Morning prayer and individual meditation time
9:45	Small-group session 1
10:45	Break
11:00	Small-group session 2
12:00	Lunch
12:45	Individual meditation time (silence in the entire area)
1:30	Free time
4:30	Worship groups prepare for Sunday worship
5:30	Dinner
6:30	Small-group session 3
8:00	Prayer stations and evening worship
10:00	Everyone in his or her room
11:00	Lights out

Sunday

8:00	Breakfast
9:00	Morning prayers and individual meditation
10:00	Student-led worship
11:30	Lunch
12:00	Departure

SAMPLE SCHEDULE FOR A MINI-RETREAT, OR LOCK-IN

Friday

6:30	Arrive, settle in
7:00	Group orientation, mailboxes
7:45	Get-acquainted games
8:15	Break, snacks
8:30	Small-group session (Introduce the topic)
9:00	Large-group activity: game or scavenger hunt
10:30	Evening devotions, singing
11:00	Quiet time
11:30	Sleep time

Saturday

8:30	Breakfast
9:00	Morning prayers, individual meditation time
9:30	Go home

CD-ROM Contents

LOCK-INS

Seven of the retreats have been shortened to lock-in-style mini-retreats. Look for them in the Lock-ins folder.

MASTER SUPPLIES LISTS

Each retreat has its own master supplies list to print out and take to the store.

HANDOUTS

Each retreat and lock-in has several reproducible handouts. Instead of having to lay this book on a copier, you can just print them from the CD-ROM.

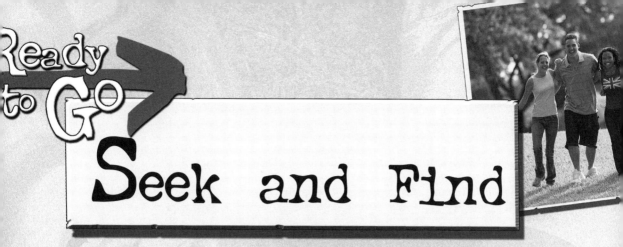

Seek and Find

Focus: The Bible tells us to seek and find God. This retreat shows youth new ways to seek God's presence and to practice habits for spiritual growth.

Key Scripture: "You will seek me and find me when you seek me with all your heart" (Jeremiah 29:13, NIV).

Options: Choose any or all of the options below, which are intended to fit into whatever schedule you create for your retreat. Make copies of the individual meditations (on CD-ROM), and hand them out before or after breakfast this morning. Feel free to add any ideas or rituals that are unique to your group.

→ First-Evening Group Devotions

→ Large-Group Session 1: Searching for Words

→ Large-Group Session 2: Seeking God

→ Large-Group Session 3: Searching for Your Small Group

→ Small-Group Session 1: Searching for God Inside Me

→ Small-Group Session 2: Searching for God

→ Second-Evening Group Devotions

→ Small-Group Session 3: Searching-for-Christ Treasure Hunt

→ Seek-and-Find Prayer Stations

Reproducible Handouts (on CD-ROM)

→ Psalm 139 Litany

→ Psalm 52 Litany

→ Searching for God

→ Seek-and-Find Treasure Hunt Reproducible Page

→ First-Morning Individual Meditation

→ Second-Morning Individual Meditation

→ Seek-and-Find Prayer Stations

FIRST-EVENING GROUP DEVOTIONS
(30 minutes)

Supplies needed: one copy of Psalm 139 Litany (on CD-ROM) per youth

Have some group singing time. Start with some fun songs your kids love to sing. If you know "Seek Ye First," include it in your selections.

Have an easy-to-sing, meditative song as a retreat theme song that you'll sing every time you gather. Sometimes it's better to find a new song that the youth have not already associated with some time or event; when the youth get to sing the song in the future, it will bring back memories of this retreat.

After some singing time, invite the youth to expect that God will communicate with them and to listen for God's small, still voice in their heart; invite them to experience God and to know that God is seeking them.

Introduce a period of silence by saying: "Quiet yourself before God. Rest in God's presence." After some silence, sing together the theme song.

Ask: "Why are you here? (Pause for silence.) What are you searching for? (Pause for silence.) What do you seek?" Pause for silence.

Hand out copies of the litany based on Psalm 139. Read the litany together. Tell the left side of the group to read Left, and the right side of the group to read Right.

LARGE-GROUP SESSION 1:
SEARCHING FOR WORDS
(20–30 minutes)

Supplies needed: markers, paper, masking tape or thumbtacks, and photos or pictures (optional)

Preparation: Before the session, write each of the following phrases on a separate sheet of paper if you do not have photos or pictures: *mountain top, icicle, milk and cookies, surf crashing on the beach, a dark cave, roaring fire, flickering candle, autumn leaf, rainy day, steady stream, a rosebud, a seed buried in the ground,* and *sunshine streaming through the forest.* Choose as many phrases as you wish. If you have photos or pictures, you can substitute them for the phrases. Post the phrases (or pictures) around the room.

Have a volunteer read **Matthew 7:7** (ask, seek, knock).

Then have the group join you in an opening prayer. Use your own words, or read the following prayer:

> Jesus, you told us that you are the way. When we feel lost and can't seem to find the path, it is good to know that you are the way. We need direction in finding how to live. On this retreat, help us to sincerely seek you. Thank you for your promise that if we seek you we will find you. Guide our way. Amen.

Next, tell the youth to walk around the room and read all of the words (or look at all of the pictures). Then tell them to choose a statement on the wall that most expresses their faith journey today and to stand by that sheet. If others are standing at the same place, have them tell one another why they chose that particular image. If no one is at the same sheet, instruct the youth to move to the closest person and explain their choice.

LARGE-GROUP SESSION 2: SEEKING GOD (20–30 minutes)

Supplies needed: a large, empty room void of chairs and tables. If it isn't totally dark, you will need blindfolds (which could be three-inch-wide strips of old sheets, long enough to tie around your head). Use this activity to introduce the topic of seeking God and to build community. Secretly appoint one person to be "God," and tell him or her to stand in one place and not to speak during the game.

Tell the youth to put on their blindfolds and walk slowly around the room while asking, "Are you God?" Tell them that when they don't get a response from someone, they will know they have found "God" and should remove their blindfolds and stand quietly next to "God" without speaking.

After the game, ask:

➜ What was it like before you found God? (Answers may include *dark, noisy,* and *confusing.*)

➜ What was it like after everyone found God? (Answers may include *light, quiet, calm,* and *close.*)

➜ How did everyone find God? (through one another)

LARGE-GROUP SESSION 3:
SEARCHING FOR YOUR SMALL GROUP
(10 minutes)

Supplies needed: a large-piece puzzle (or a photo you don't mind cutting up) per small group, a pen, scissors, glue, and construction paper (optional)

Preparation: For each small group, write one group member's name on the front of each puzzle piece. If you don't have a puzzle, glue a photo to a piece of construction paper. Write out this Scripture verse on back of the photo or on the reverse side of the completed puzzle:

> You will seek me and find me when you seek me with all your heart.

> (Jeremiah 29:13, NIV)

If you are using a photo, cut it into as many pieces as there are members of the small group.

Put all of the puzzle pieces in one pile, mix them up, and lay them out on a table, with the names' side up. Each person is to find his or her name then find others who are part of the same puzzle. This method is how they find the members of their small groups. When each small group's members have found one another, ask them to put their puzzle together. Have them look on the back side of the puzzle to find the Scripture for the day. Challenge all of the youth to memorize it.

SMALL-GROUP SESSION 1:
SEARCHING FOR GOD INSIDE ME
(30 minutes)

Supplies needed: a piece of paper for per youth, markers or pens, and Bibles

Instruct each person to write his or her first name vertically down the left margin of the paper. Invite the teens to construct acrostics (poems with each line beginning with a successive letter of a word, thus spelling out a word). For their acrostics, the youth should use words that describe their personalities, traits, and abilities. Here is an example:

Smart
Ambitious
Musical

Allow time for completion of this task; then have the youth tell their small group about their acrostics.

When everyone has talked, have the group set all of the papers down where everyone can look at them. Ask the groups to work together to do another acrostic for each of their names but to use characteristics of or names for God. For example:

Sustainer
Awesome
Mighty

Ask:

→ What does this activity symbolize?

→ How do you experience God in others?

→ In what way does the nature of God reveal itself in you?

Have some youth read the following Scriptures out loud: **1 Timothy 4:14; Colossians 1:27; Philippians 2:13;** and **Philippians 1:6.** Ask:

→ How do these verses enlighten your understanding of having a relationship with God?

→ What do they tell you about the nature of God? about your relationship with God?

→ What feelings did you have when you heard these verses?

→ If you took them to heart, how would they make a difference in the way you thought about yourself? about others?

SMALL-GROUP SESSION 2: SEARCHING FOR GOD
(30 minutes)

Supplies needed: pens, one copy of Searching for God handout (on CD-ROM) for each youth, a CD of meditative music, and a CD player

Distribute the Searching for God handouts. Invite each person to write or draw in the corresponding pie slices what name they use for God and why, what color they think describes God, a symbol that represents their relationship with God, an image in nature that describes God, and a song that makes them feel close to God.

Next, play meditative background music and read the following Scriptures:

> O Lord, our Sovereign,
>   how majestic is your name in all the earth!
> You have set your glory about the heavens. . . .
>
> When I look at your heavens, the work of your fingers,
> the moon and the stars that you have established;
> what are human beings that you are mindful of them?
>   (Psalm 8:1, 3-4a)
>
> The LORD is my rock, my fortress, and my deliverer,
> my God, my rock in whom I take refuge,
> my shield and the horn of my salvation, my stronghold.
>   (Psalm 18:1-2)
>
> The Lord is my shepherd, I shall not want.
> He makes me lie down in green pastures;
> He leads me beside still waters.
>   (Psalm 23:1-2)
>
> The Lord is my light, my salvation;
> whom shall I fear?
>   (Psalm 27:1a)
>
> As an eagle stirs up its nest, and hovers over its young;
> as it spreads its wings, takes them up,
>   and bears them aloft on its pinions,
> the LORD alone guided him.
>   (Deuteronomy 32:11-12a)
>
> As a mother comforts her child,
>   so I will comfort you.
>   (Isaiah 66:13a)

Allow each person an opportunity to show his or her circle and interpret it for the small group. Add these circles to the altar in your worship space.

SECOND-EVENING GROUP DEVOTIONS
(20-30 minutes)

Supplies needed: copies of Psalm 52 Litany (on CD-ROM)

Sing some more of your favorite songs. Silly songs are always fun on a retreat.

After some singing, invite the youth to expect that God will communicate with them and to listen for God's small, still voice in their hearts. Tell the students that God is seeking them. Say: "Quiet yourself before God. Rest in God's presence."

Sing your theme song and "Seek Ye First."

Ask: "Where do you seek forgiveness? (Pause for silence.) From whom do you need forgiveness?" (Pause for silence.)

Hand out copies of litany based on Psalm 52. Read the litany together. The left side of the room reads Left, and the right side of the group reads Right.

SMALL-GROUP SESSION 3:
SEEK-AND-FIND TREASURE HUNT
(60 minutes)

Supplies needed: nine plastic Easter eggs per small group, one bag (with handles) for each small group, colored masking tape (optional), one copy of Seek-and-Find Treasure Hunt handout (on CD-ROM) per group, and a bag for each group.

Preparation: Assign one egg color to each small group. (If you have more groups than colors, use colored masking tape to differentiate the groups' eggs. For example, one group might look for yellow eggs while another group looks for yellow eggs that have a blue masking-tape band around them.) Cut the handout's slips apart, and insert a slip into each egg, making sure each group receives all nine of the statement slips. Hide the eggs within a defined parameter.

Say to everyone: "Each group has nine eggs to find. Your group will be given a bag and told what color of eggs to search for. Do not disturb eggs that belong to other groups.

"When you have found all of your nine eggs, go inside and open them one at a time. As a small group, answer the questions and talk about what you found in the eggs. Each egg contains something we find when we search for Christ."

Tell each group what color or design of eggs to search for, and define the boundaries for this activity. Then send the youth out to find the eggs.

SEEK-AND-FIND PRAYER STATIONS
(60 minutes)

Supplies needed: Seek-and-Find Prayer Station handouts (on CD-ROM), a pen and a piece of paper for each youth, six small tables or six large plastic storage bins, cloth to cover each table or storage bin, and six candles. (If you don't have material, you can find old sheets, bedspreads, or tablecloths at thrift stores and cut them so that they cover several tables.)

Preparation: Spread the tables or storage bins around the room. Cover each of them with cloth, and put a candle on them. Put each prayer-station handout by its corresponding station.

Have a time of prayer around the stations. Tell the group your hopes and dreams for them as they learn to seek and find God. Have a brief time of singing; then let the youth travel through the prayer stations at their own pace. Close the retreat with whatever ritual you use to close your youth meetings.

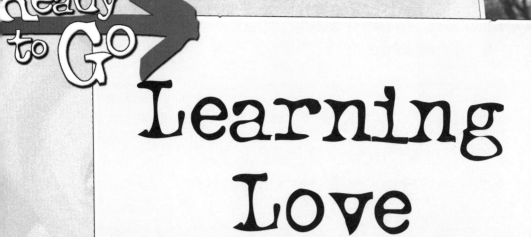

Learning Love

Focus: to develop teens' understanding of how to genuinely love others and experience God's love

Key Scripture: "Beloved, let us love one another, because love is from God; everyone who loves is born of God and knows God" (1 John 4:7).

Choose from any or all of the listed options to create your retreat. Make copies of the individual meditations (on CD-ROM), and hand them out before or after breakfast each morning.

Options
→ Evening Group Devotions
→ Large-Group Activity 1: Identifying Love's Languages
→ Large-Group Activity 2: Love-Language Skits
→ Small-Group Activity 1: Love-Language Posters
→ Small-Group Activity 2: In-Depth Discussion
→ Small-Group Activity 3: Love Scriptures
→ Prayer Stations

Reproducible Handouts (on CD-ROM)
→ Love's Languages
→ Love's Languages Scoring Sheet
→ Small-Group Activity 2
→ Love Scriptures
→ First-Morning Individual Meditation
→ Second-Morning Individual Meditation
→ Prayer Stations

EVENING GROUP DEVOTIONS
(30-45 minutes)

Supplied needed: a Bible

Begin your group devotions with some of your group's favorite songs. (Silly songs are always a fun way to start.) If you know "Open the Eyes of My Heart," include it in your selections.

Also, choose a theme song for the retreat. Your youth will attach memories of this retreat to the song, so that when they hear it in the future they will remember this trip.

Next, invite the youth to expect that God will communicate with them and to listen for God's still, small voice in their heart; invite them to experience God's love.

Allow a few minutes of silence.

Say: "Quiet yourself before God. Rest in God's presence. Ask God to open the eyes of your heart." Sing "Open the Eyes of My Heart."

Have a volunteer read **Romans 8:35-39.**

Introduction: Now give an introduction that is interactive, with the participants answering your questions. Read the following introduction to the youth, or put it in your own words:

"Well, Paul certainly covers it all in those verses—persecution, angels, death, rulers, and the future. It feels like he's trying to make a strong point, doesn't it? It seems that comprehending, understanding, and experiencing God's love is important.

"Sword, famine, and peril sound like nasty stuff. But many things, people, and situations cause me to doubt God's love for me. They aren't as awful as the things Paul describes, but they still get in the way of receiving God's love. What are some things that separate us from God's love? Why, do you think, does this separation occur?

"I think I'm the one who separates myself from God; I don't think God moves away from me. God's choice is always love, as Paul says in Romans.

"I don't always choose love. I want to, but sometimes it seems too difficult, unfair, and unreasonable. It requires that I forgive someone who has hurt me. It requires that I care about 'the least of these.' It won't allow me to be selfish, unkind, apathetic, or greedy."

Instructions: Say, "I'm going to read off some half-sentences. When I read one, turn to a person and say what first comes to mind. You will have a couple of minutes to talk to each other for each partial sentence.

"When I separate myself from God's love, I ..."

Give the pairs a few minutes to talk. Then say: "Now turn to a different person and complete this sentence: When I stay connected to God's love, I ..."

When the conversation is dying down, get the teens' attention and invite them to spend a few more minutes in silence, meditating on the love of Christ and opening their hearts to God.

Ask the group to join hands; close with this prayer or one of your own: "Dear God whose nature is love: Thank you for promising that nothing can change your love for me. I'm thankful that there is nothing I can do to increase or decrease your love for me. I need to work on increasing my love for you and for others. I don't like myself when I separate myself from your love. Help me to connect with you. Fill me with your love, which enables me to be the best me in the world. Thank you for never giving up on anyone. Amen."

LARGE-GROUP ACTIVITY 1: IDENTIFYING LOVE'S LANGUAGES (60 minutes)

Supplies needed: pens for each person, and one copy of Love's Languages handout and of Love's Languages Scoring Sheet (on CD-ROM) per youth

Introduction: Read the following introduction, or put it in your own words: "Love is pretty important. Scripture tells us that God *is* love. It also says that the greatest commandment is to love your neighbor as yourself. You begin living out that commandment by accepting God's love for you; next, you love yourself so that you can love others.

"Love is always a choice. When you choose to love, you are choosing to follow Christ and to become part of the world's solution instead of part of its problems.

"Love isn't really something that comes naturally—it challenges us to reach out to others instead of just focusing on ourselves. Dr. Gary Chapman has written several books on the languages of love. He teaches that love expresses itself in five different ways: words of affirmation and affection, physical touch, quality time, acts of service, and gifts.

"Dr. Chapman thinks that each of us has one or two preferred ways in which we receive love. To be the best at loving others, we should discover their preferred love languages and respond appropriately. Once a person is receiving love in his or her two preferred languages, then the gestures of love in other languages become more meaningful."

Instructions: Distribute Love's Languages handouts. Say: "Now we're going to do an exercise that will help you discover your preferred love languages. On the Love's Languages handout, each section has five statements. For each section, give five points to the sentence that best describes the way you say I love you. Give your second preference four points, your third preference three points, your fourth preference two points, and your last preference one point."

Allow the youth adequate time to complete this task. When they are done, hand out the Scoring Sheets. Ask the teens to add up their scores and to circle their two highest scores.

Say: "This exercise was intended to help you determine your preferred styles of receiving, and probably giving, love. At the bottom of the scoring sheet are the five love languages, or ways we give and receive love."

Ask each person to relay what their two highest areas are and say if they think these areas are the two ways they most like receiving love. Some teens might have equal scores in several areas; ask those youth to tell why they like receiving love in the two manners.

Ask:

➔ What new information have you learned through this activity?

➔ What have you learned about yourself?

➔ What have you learned about understanding other people?

➔ How will you use this information to improve your relationships with others?

LARGE-GROUP ACTIVITY 2: LOVE-LANGUAGE SKITS (45 minutes)

Divide the group into partners who have similar love-language preferences. (If you have an odd number of youth, three youth can form a group.) Instruct each pair to create a skit demonstrating some examples of giving love in their preferred language. Allow the students ten minutes to prepare; then invite each pair to present its roleplay to the group.

Ask:

➔ Are there some times when you prefer one love language over another? If so, can you give a brief example?

➔ Do you receive love differently than other people? (Again, ask for brief examples.)

SMALL-GROUP ACTIVITY 1: LOVE-LANGUAGE POSTERS (30 minutes)

Supplies needed: markers, five sheets of paper for each small group, one sheet of posterboard per small group, glue, scissors, and magazines

Preparation: On the top of each sheet of paper, write one of the five love languages (words of affirmation and affection, quality time, touch, acts of service, and gifts).

Have the small groups write on the respective sheets of paper as many examples as they can think of for each of the five love languages and add pictures from magazines that represent this language. (If you must, remind the youth that it would be inappropriate to include anything lewd or rude.) Next, have the students put these five pieces of paper on the posterboard to create a poster about how to love.

The groups should all sign the posters and hang them in the meeting room or around the altar for display.

SMALL-GROUP ACTIVITY 2: IN-DEPTH DISCUSSION
(30 minutes)

Supplies needed: Bibles, pens, and a copy of Small-Group Activity 2 handout (on CD-ROM) for each member of your group

Read 1 John 3:11-18. Have the groups discuss this question: What does this Scripture mean to you?

Next, have each person complete Small-Group Activity 2 handout. Give the students adequate time to talk, reflect, and write.

Handout 2 asks the teens to complete the following sentences:

➜ One way in which I showed someone that I loved him or her this week was ...

➜ I would really like it if someone did this to say, "I love you":

Bring the small groups back together, and have them discuss these questions:

➜ What did you learn about yourself from this exercise?

➜ What was easy to write about or reflect on? What was difficult?

➜ Was the way you showed love your preferred style, or do you think it was the recipient's preferred style?

➜ Think about what you wrote for the second question. What person or persons could express love for you in this way?

➜ Think of one of the persons you just named. What do you think he or she would ask for answering the same question?

SMALL-GROUP ACTIVITY 3: LOVE SCRIPTURES
(20 minutes)

Supplies needed: an envelope for each small group, a marker, and one copy of the Love Scriptures handout (on CD-ROM) per youth

Preparation: Label the envelopes, "Love Scriptures"; cut apart the love Scriptures on each handout, and put all of them into an envelope.

Give each group an envelope. Ask them to pass it around, with each person taking out a slip of paper. Like the slips of paper in fortune cookies, these messages are meant to be their personal Scripture and promise.

Before you read the closing prayer, go around the circle and invite the students to offer a one-sentence prayer based on the Scripture they drew from the envelope. They might say, for example, "Help me to remember that you love me, and I can trust my future with you" or "Thank you for being a loving and forgiving God." They could also just read their Scripture to the whole group.

Have the youth join hands in a prayer circle. Close by reading the following prayer, or say your own: "May the God of love fill you with all joy and peace as you trust in God, so that you may overflow with love by the power of the Holy Spirit."

PRAYER STATIONS
(60 minutes)

Supplies needed: Learning-Love Prayer Station handouts (on CD-ROM); additional supplies are listed on the handout.

Preparation: Spread the tables or storage bins around the room. Cover each of them with cloth, and put a candle on them. Put each prayer-station handout by its corresponding station.

Have a time of singing; then tell the youth they can pray at their own pace around any of the stations.

Grace and the Good Shepherd

Focus: The youth will grow in their understanding of grace as experienced through stories about the Good Shepherd.

Key Scripture: "For by grace you have been saved through faith, and this is not your own doing; it is the gift of God" (Ephesians 2:8).

Organize the options to fit your schedule. In between the options, allow the youth to do the individual meditations (which require Bibles) and the prayer walks (on CD-ROM). Give fifteen to thirty minutes for these periods of meditation.

Options
→ Opening Worship

→ Opening Group Game: Here Sheep, Here Sheep

→ Small-Group Activity 1: Good-Shepherd Want Ads

→ Small-Group Activity 2: The Gift of Grace

→ Small-Group Activity 3: Bible Study on Luke 15:3-7

→ Small-Group Activity 4: Lying in Green Pastures

→ Large-Group Activity 1: I Once Was Lost

→ Large-Group Activity 2: *Grace Competition*—an Oxymoron

→ Large-Group Activity 3: What's Grace Got to Do With It?

→ Large-Group Activity 4: The Good Shepherd Seeks the Lost

→ Large-Group Activity 5: Wheel of Fortune Games

→ Closing Worship

Reproducible Handouts (on CD-ROM)
→ Opening Worship

→ Survivor

→ Discussion Guide for Luke

→ Lying in Green Pastures Discussion Guide

→ What's Grace Got to Do With It?

→ Grace Timeline

→ Wheel of Fortune

→ Closing-Worship Reproducible Pages

→ First-Morning Individual Meditation

→ Second-Morning Individual Meditation

→ Individual Prayer Walks 1, 2, and 3

OPENING WORSHIP
(30 minutes)

Supplies needed: a copy of Opening Worship handout (on CD-ROM) per youth, and a copy of Survivor handout (on CD-ROM) for each actor

Distribute the Opening Worship handouts; assign Voices 1, 2, 3, and 4; and have the youth read through the litany. Then assign roles for the "Survivor" skit, give each actor a copy of the handout, and have them act out the skit.

Close by reading the psalm and, with the youth, reading the closing prayer.

OPENING GROUP GAME:
HERE SHEEP, HERE SHEEP
(at least 45 minutes)

Supplies needed: blindfolds for half your group; strips of paper; pens or pencils; and a hat, bowl, or bag

For this exercise in name learning, divide the youth into two groups: the sheep and the shepherds. Distribute pens or pencils and slips of paper to the sheep. Have each sheep write his or her name on a piece of paper and put it in a hat, bowl, or bag. Blindfold all of the sheep, and gather them together in the center of the room. If you can, dim the lights.

Next, have the shepherds draw the sheep's names from the container and stand in a large circle around the sheep; privately tell the shepherds that they are to quietly call their sheep by name. If a sheep other than their own comes to them, they should gently herd him or her back into the center of the circle. When a sheep finds his or her shepherd, the shepherd should remove the sheep's blindfold and stand in the circle with him or her.

Instruct the sheep to "bah" loudly and try to find their personal shepherd.

When everyone has found his or her sheep or shepherd, have the pairs sit facing each other. Ask them to discuss the questions below. Read one question at a time out loud, and give the youth a few moments to discuss each question before you read the next question. Ask:

→ Sheep, how easy or difficult was this game for you?

→ Shepherds, how did you feel about this activity?

→ Did some pairs find each other more quickly than others? If so, why?

→ What contributed to the difficulty of finding each other?

→ What might this game have to do with Christ, the Good Shepherd, seeking us?

Ask for a show of hands from those who found their partner quickly. Invite a couple of them to relate what helped them find each other.

Next, ask for a show of hands from those who had a lot of difficulty finding their partner. Invite a couple of them to report what contributed to the difficulty of finding each other.

Lastly, ask a couple of youth to talk about what they think this game had to do with Christ as the shepherd and us as sheep.

SMALL-GROUP ACTIVITY 1: GOOD-SHEPHERD WANT ADS
(30-45 minutes)

Supplies needed: markers, posterboard, paper, colored pencils, and newsprint

Have the small groups make want ads for the Good Shepherd. The youth should show enduring qualities of God, using words or pictures. These ads could be a poster describing the nature of the Good Shepherd. Or, the teens could draw on a large sheet of newsprint the outline of a group member and fill in the outline by writing God's shepherdlike characteristics.

Bring the small groups together, and ask one member of each group to present its want ad, providing details and explanations.

SMALL-GROUP ACTIVITY 2: THE GIFT OF GRACE
(45 minutes)

Supplies needed: party hat per youth; paper; markers; gift stickers that say, "To" and "From" ; and Bibles

Hand out party hats, and ask everyone to put them on. Distribute paper, markers, and gift tags or stickers. Start this activity by reading the following introduction, or put it in your own words: "I love parties, especially when they are meant for me. People throw parties for birthdays and graduations and for when you get married, have a baby, get promoted, or move. Parties mean good food, friends, and, potentially, presents. Can you remember your favorite party?

"Now think about the best gift you've ever received. It could have been at a party or not. What was the absolute best gift ever? Draw a picture of the gift; on the gift sticker, write who gave it to you." Give the youth about five minutes to prepare the pictures.

Invite each person to talk with the group about their drawings and tell why this gift was the best.

Have the group discuss these questions:

→ What made this gift special?
→ Why do you highly value this gift?
→ Was it the most extravagant gift you ever received?
→ Can you tell us something about the person who gave it to you.

When the conversation dies down, distribute the Bibles and have the small groups read **Ephesians 2:8**. They should talk about what the verse is saying and discuss how their faith would be different if they had to earn grace.

SMALL-GROUP ACTIVITY 3: BIBLE STUDY ON LUKE 15:3-7
(50 minutes)

Supplies needed: copies of the Discussion Guide for Luke:15:3-7 (on CD-ROM) for each youth, Bibles, pens, newsprint, a posterboard, and several markers

Distribute newsprint and markers. Before the groups read the Scripture, have them try to piece together what they remember about the parable of the lost sheep. One member of each group should take notes on a sheet of newsprint.

Now hand out the Bibles and read aloud to the groups the story found in **Luke 15:3-7**.

Ask: "Whom did you most relate to in this story as you listened? Raise your hand if you found yourself connecting with the Good Shepherd. Raise your hand if you thought of yourself as the lost sheep. How many of you thought of yourself as one of the sheep back with the herd?"

Distribute copies of Discussion Guide for Luke 15:3-7, and have the small groups talk through the questions. When the discussion is dying down, ask the groups to report what their answers to the last question were.

SMALL-GROUP ACTIVITY 4: LYING IN GREEN PASTURES
(30–45 minutes)

Supplies needed: a Bible, copies of Lying-in-Green-Pastures Discussion Guide (on CD-ROM)

Read **Psalm 23:1-2** to the group. Ask: "What do we know about sheep? Has anyone ever raised sheep? Does anyone know how to make sheep lie down?"

Say: "The twenty-third psalm is a popular Scripture that describes the relationship between the Shepherd (God) and the sheep (us). Shepherding sheep was a common livelihood at the time this psalm was written. Nowadays, the meaning can get lost on us, because most of us know little about sheep. We need to know that it is almost impossible to make sheep lie down unless they are free from all fear, friction with other sheep, pests, and hunger. It is up to the shepherd to eliminate these factors so that the sheep will lie down."

Read **2 Timothy 1:7** to the group. Then distribute Lying-in-Green-Pastures Discussion Guide and have the small groups talk through it.

LARGE-GROUP ACTIVITY 1: I ONCE WAS LOST
(at least 20 minutes)

Supplies needed: magazines (preferably about nature and adventure), scissors, thumbtacks or masking tape, markers, large sheets of paper (such as newsprint), and a Bible

Preparation: Cut out magazine photos that portray desolate and bleak-looking places. Look for cold or dark, barren scenes. Affix these photos, as well as large sheets of paper, to the walls. Put some markers under each piece of paper.

Lead the group in singing the first verse of "Amazing Grace." Then have a volunteer read **Luke 15:3-7.**

Invite the youth to look at the photos, and encourage them to write words or draw pictures on the large sheet of paper that describe what it feels like to be lost. (For instance, the teens may think of song lyrics that express being lost.)

Next, instruct the youth to choose a partner to talk with about what it feels like to be lost.

After enough talk time, gather everyone together in a circle. Ask each person to either read from or describe one of the sheets of paper or to explain the feeling of being lost.

Close this exercise by singing again the first verse of "Amazing Grace."

LARGE-GROUP ACTIVITY 2: GRACE COMPETITION—AN OXYMORON (30 minutes)

Supplies needed: a pen and piece of paper for each small group, small prizes for each group, and service bells (optional)

Gather the entire group together. Have the small groups sit together in tight circles, and give a pen and piece of paper to each small group. Say: "I will read a definition of a word. When your group knows the word, write it on your piece of paper and send a runner to bring the answer to me. The first team to bring me the word gets ten points." You may wish to use service bells for them to ring.

Here are the definitions to read aloud:

→ a prayer said before a meal (answer = grace)

→ having or showing kindness and compassion (answer = gracious)

→ lacking any sense of what is proper (answer = graceless)

→ Spanish for "thank you" (answer = *gracias*)

→ having beauty of form and movement (answer = graceful)

→ thankful appreciation for things received (answer = gratitude)

→ accepting a gift with politeness (answer = gracious)

→ a tip added to the cost for good service (answer = gratuity)

→ a delay for the payment of a debt (answer = grace)

→ a person who does not appreciate a kindness (answer = ingrate)

→ an expression of astonishment (answer = Goodness gracious!)

→ the way to address an archbishop, duke, or duchess (answer = Your Grace)

→ something given free of charge (answer = gratis)

→ goodwill or favor (answer = grace)

→ a note in small type that serves as an embellishment in a piece of music (answer = grace note)

→ to be in the favor of someone (answer = in good graces)

→ the love and favor of God toward humankind (answer = grace)

To show an example of grace, give prizes to everyone, not just the "winners."

LARGE-GROUP ACTIVITY 3: WHAT'S GRACE GOT TO DO WITH IT?
(20 minutes)

Supplies needed: a pen per youth and a copy of What's Grace Got to Do With It? handout (on CD-ROM) for each person

Distribute the handouts and the pens. Instruct each youth to check each item he or she has used or purchased in the past week.

Now tell the youth to circle each checked item that they had to earn or pay for completely by themselves. Each person should tally the number of such items. Then each person should tally the number of items that he or she received free. Ask for volunteers to relay to the group their tallies.

Say: "We take most of these things for granted, forgetting that for over half the youth in the world, some of these things are not available. Many people go to bed hungry every night. Even the act of being grateful for things we often taken for granted can open our hearts to God's gift of grace."

Ask the group to name things God freely gives. After each person names something, instruct the group to respond, "We give you thanks, Lord."

LARGE-GROUP ACTIVITY 4:
THE GOOD SHEPHERD SEEKS THE LOST
(30–45 minutes)

Supplies needed: paper, pens or markers, and copies of Grace Timeline handout (on CD-ROM)

Say: "God is active in our lives all the time. God is the source of life, the ground of our being. God acts in the world in ordinary circumstances. God is the Good Shepherd who seeks us when we are lost. This seeking nature of God is also known as prevenient grace, which is God at work in our lives before we are aware of it or acknowledge it. God gives us this grace freely, waiting for us to respond. Our response to and acceptance of God's grace is called justification by faith.

"John Wesley used a house metaphor to describe these types of graces. He compared prevenient grace to God bringing us to the porch of God's house. Justifying grace is saying yes and walking through the door. Sanctifying grace is making God's house your home."

Distribute the pens or markers and the Grace Timeline handouts. Have the youth read the instructions and work individually on their timelines. Remind the teens that this activity is for themselves and that they do not have to let anyone else see their paper.

When the students have finished, gather the group and ask:

→ What did you learn about yourself from this activity?

→ What is one thing you identified as God's prevenient grace working in your life?

→ Can anyone describe a moment when you said yes to God's grace? What did this experience mean to you?

→ Can someone reveal one of his or her dreams about what it would be like to live fully in God's grace and presence?

LARGE-GROUP ACTIVITY 5: WHEEL OF FORTUNE

Supplies needed: sheets of newsprint or other paper; pens; small pieces of paper; markers; spinners from old board games (one for each small group); Bibles (optional); copies of Wheel of Fortune handout (on CD-ROM) and tape or thumbtacks to attach the sheets to a wall, OR sturdy objects to prop the paper up against, such as easels

Preparation: On sheets of newsprint or large sheets of paper, you will be drawing blanks that stand for letters the students are to guess (as in the game of hangman or *Wheel of Fortune*).

Start with the first phrase. Count how many small groups are on your retreat, and divide that number in half. (You may have to combine groups if you have an odd number of groups.) The quotient you get is the number of sheets you will need for the first phrase. (For instance, if you have eight small groups, you will need four game sheets.)

Now draw a blank for each of the letters in the following phrase, putting a space between words:

NO PAIN, NO GAIN (_ _ _ _ _ _, _ _ _ _ _ _)

At the top of the sheet, label it "Phrase 1."

After you have prepared the first-phrase game sheets, gather the same number of sheets as you did for the first phrase and draw blanks for this phrase:

I INSIST ON MY RIGHTS

At the top of the sheets, label them "Phrase 2."

For the third phrase, go through the same process, with the same number of sheets, labeled "Phrase 3":

THE EARLY BIRD GETS THE WORM

For phrase four (below), you'll need to prepare half the number of sheets. (So if you were preparing four for each phrase, you'll need two.)

YOU GET WHAT YOU PAY FOR

For the final three phrases, you will need only one sheet per phrase:

WHAT GOES AROUND COMES AROUND

THERE'S NO SUCH THING AS A FREE LUNCH

I WANT WHAT I DESERVE, NOTHING MORE, NOTHING LESS

Label these final game sheets "Phrase 5," "Phrase 6," and "Phrase 7."

Inform the adult volunteers about their role as hosts in the game. For each volunteer counselor, write down on a small piece of paper the answer to each mystery phrase, and give these answers to the volunteer. Also give each leader a copy of the Wheel of Fortune Handout, which will help them determine which team goes first.

Make sure the spinners have a number in each slice of its circle; if not, tape on the spinners pieces of paper with numbers written on them.

Put the sheets on display in your meeting space, either by affixing them to a wall or by propping each one on an easel. Make sure each Phrase 1 sheet is close to a Phrase 2 and 3 sheet.

Game time: Distribute the Bibles. Pair up each small group with another small group, and tell the youth their "partner group" is their opposing team. Give each pair of groups a spinner, and have the groups gather around the sheet labeled "Phrase 1." Have the adult volunteers stand by a sheet to write the correct letters guessed and tally points on the sheet.

Say: "We're going to play a letter-guessing game. But before we can start, we need to determine which team can go first. Your leader will read out part of a Bible verse. The first team that finishes the verse will get to go first."

After the leaders have determined which team can go first, say: "Now let's get to the game. Each team will compete against its opposing team to guess letters, as in the game show *Wheel of Fortune*. When it's your team's turn, your team will spin the spinner. Whatever number you land on is the number of points you will win if you guess a letter correctly. If your team guesses a letter correctly, you can spin again and guess another letter. Your team will keep guessing letters until it guesses one that is not on the game sheet; then it's your opposing team's turn. Whichever team scores the most points for the first three phrases moves on to the next round. Here's a hint for these phrases and sayings: They do *not* reflect a theology of grace; they are the opposite of grace."

After the first round, have each winning group compete against another group for Phrase 4, using the Wheel of Fortune handout to determine which team can go first. Then those groups who won can compete to go first then compete to win Phrases 5, 6, and 7. The team that wins the last round is the winning team.

CLOSING WORSHIP

Supplies needed: one print-out of each Closing-Worship handout (on CD-ROM), thumbtacks or masking tape, pocket-sized notebooks, pens, worship CDs, and a CD player

Preparation: Print each of the Closing-Worship handouts, enlarging them as much as possible. These posters include the definitions of Wesley's three types of grace, as well as the following Scriptures:

- Acts 20:24
- Romans 1:6
- Romans 3:23-24
- Romans 5:1-3
- Romans 6:14
- Romans 6:15
- 1 Corinthians 1:4-5
- 2 Corinthians 6:1
- 2 Corinthians 9:14-15
- Galatians 5:4
- Ephesians 1:6
- Ephesians 2:8
- 1 Timothy 1:14
- 2 Timothy 1:9
- Titus 2:11

On the walls in your meeting or worship area, post the Closing-Worship handouts.

Closing-worship time: Sing hymns or worship songs about grace. Suggestions include "Amazing Grace," "Come, Thou Fount of Every Blessing," and "Grace Flows Down."

Now play some worship music as background music. Give each person a small notebook. Invite the youth to spend time at each Scripture poster, copying the Scripture into their notebook, and rewriting in their notebook the Scripture in their own words.

Invite volunteers to read their passage and their paraphrase. Close with prayer.

Light Your Soul Fire

Focus: to help youth light or reignite their "soul fire" for God

Key Scripture: "And how do you benefit if you gain the whole world but lose your own soul?" (Mark 8:36, NLT).

Organize the options to fit your schedule, but have the students do the individual meditations (which require Bibles) before Small-Group Exercise: Being Present.

Options
→ Opening-Night Experience

→ Small-Group Exercise: Interaction

→ Interaction Exercise: Faith Blessings

→ Small-Group Exercise: Being Present

→ Deliberation Exercise: Beggar Beads

→ Small-Group Discussion: Celebration

→ Celebration Exercise: Party Planners

→ Small-Group Exercise: Consideration and Being Kind

→ Consideration Exercise: Care Cards

→ Small-Group Exercise: Affirmation

→ Affirmation Exercise: Affirmation Alternative

→ Closing Worship

Reproducible Handouts (on CD-ROM)
→ Individual Meditation 1, 2, and 3

→ Prayer Stations

→ Roles for Participants

OPENING-NIGHT EXPERIENCE
(30-45 minutes)

Supplies needed: paper, pens or pencils, candles, a goodie bag for each youth, a CD player or cassette player, a CD or cassette of contemplative music, matches, a Bible, and symbols of various aspects of this retreat (such as a cross, praying hands, a party hat, a small-group nametag, and a pair of shoes)

Preparation: Find worship center. (Have it indoors if the weather is unpleasant.) On the altar, place symbols of the various aspects of the retreat. Find a campsite where your group can gather around a campfire. Also, leave goodie bags with the students' names on them in the teens' respective rooms.

Singing: "As the Deer"

Scripture: Psalm 42:1-2

Introduction to theme: Go to the campfire or other worship site. Play contemplative music in the background. Give a piece of paper and a pen or pencil to each youth. Read the following paragraphs, or have a different person present each one:

> The focus of this retreat is on lighting, or restoring, your soul. Most of us are good at caring for our physical bodies. Proper diet, exercise, and rest lay the foundation for our health. Such groundwork significantly contributes to our spiritual care. In this retreat, however, we will focus on additional practices that can restore your soul. Our hope is that you will discover practical methods you'll continue to use to cultivate your spirit.

> On this retreat, we'll practice contemplation, reflection, deliberation, consideration, affirmation, meditation, and celebration. Sometimes, these practices can be done simultaneously because they reinforce one another. Some sessions will emphasize just one way to light your soul fire.

> To effectively retreat and restore our soul, we begin by shedding ourselves of any prejudices, hatred, resentments, or other negative feelings that keep us from renewal. Each of you was given a piece of paper. Write on the paper whatever you need to give up or surrender to God to make room for your spiritual growth.

> **Ephesians 4** says that to be renewed we must put away our old self that is corrupt and deluded by its lusts, put away falsehood, give up

stealing, and not let evil come out of our mouth. We must put away all bitterness, wrath, anger, wrangling, slander, vulgar talk, greed, and malice. Instead we are to be kind, tenderhearted, and forgiving. Paul calls us to be beloved children of God and live in love, as Christ loved us.

While we sing "Open the Eyes of My Heart," prayerfully come forward and throw your paper into the fire.

Sing: "Open the Eyes of My Heart"

Pray: O Lord, we begin this retreat by sincerely confessing our sins. We realize that sin is anything that gets in the way of our relationship with you. We want to love you with all of our heart, mind, and soul; but most of the time we don't. We are thankful that you are faithful even when we are not. We thank you for being forgiving and for offering to restore us when we turn to you. Bless our time together on retreat. Thank you for being here in our midst. Turn our hearts toward you. Let this retreat be an experience where we draw close to your heart so that our souls may be lit with the fire of your Spirit. Amen.

Instructions: Gather around the worship center that you have prepared ahead of time. Read aloud the instructions below. At the conclusion of each of the paragraphs, have someone light a candle to place on your altar:

Our days on retreat begin and end with specific times scheduled for contemplation and reflection. Take these times seriously; respect others by providing privacy and silence. Find a space for yourself, and open your heart to God. Honor this sacred time and space for your soul. *[Light a candle.]*

Goodie bags with your names on them have been left in your rooms. They are our way of celebrating your participation in this retreat. You are special, and we believe that God's Spirit has drawn you to this place. We know God is here and is longing to be closer to you; this retreat is an opportunity for you to draw closer to God. *[Light a candle.]*

You will be assigned to a small group tomorrow. As you meet in your group, be honest and choose to grow. You will be given the opportunity to create and imagine with others. Small groups function best when all members are accepting of one another. Christians are called to accept everyone, not just those who are like us, who agree with us, or who are easy to be with. Acceptance is not just tolerance; when we accept someone, we welcome the person and remain open to discovering who he or she is. We do not judge, attack, reject, or slam one another but find fellowship through the working of the Holy Spirit. By doing so, we may find new friends. Pray that each member of your small group will be open to God's spirit and find him- or herself in this place of acceptance and fellowship. *[Light a candle.]*

A psalmist said, "My soul waits for the Lord more than those who watch for the morning" (**Psalm 130:6a**). If we are honest, we too have resided in the darkness, waiting for the morning light. Each of us feels that empty place in our soul that desires to be healed and filled with what is most meaningful and lasting. Don't fear the struggle. Remember that God is with us in the midst of our fear and that the dark place is meant to lead you somewhere. Saint Augustine prayed in his *Confessions*, "My soul is restless until it finds its rest in Thee." In the darkness, you have companions who are also seeking the light. Through spiritual practices you are invited to find light for your soul fire. *[Light a candle.]*

This retreat is to become a place of solace and safety where we find holy ground, which can be scary but is always transforming. Moses experienced holy ground through the fire of the burning bush. He took off his shoes in recognition that he was on holy ground, in the presence of God. In awe, Moses encountered God in the burning bush. The bush was on fire, but the fire did not consume it. We invite you on this retreat to enter holy ground and to let the fire light your soul. Fire has the ability to transform, forging metals and making them stronger. But fire is risky, just as walking on Holy Ground is risky. It requires a change in us. *[Light a candle.]*

Scripture: Read Acts 7:30-34.

Say: "I invite you to take off your shoes as an act of humility and of recognition that this place may become holy ground for us. Remove your shoes, and place them behind you as an act of worship."

Sing: "Holy Ground"

Close in prayer.

SMALL-GROUP EXERCISE: INTERACTION
(45–60 minutes)

Supplies needed: a Bible

Note: Talk to your pastor or priest about what you need to do to have a Communion service to end this day on your retreat.

Begin by reading **Ephesians 4:1-7, 4:25; 5:8.**

Say: "I will read aloud some questions about this passage. Your group will have one minute in which each person will offer his or her response while the others listen."

Let the youth talk for one minute after you read each of these questions:

→ What appeals to you most about this description of how Christians should live together?

→ What prevents this way of life from happening? What gets in the way?

Say or put in your own words: "In Latin, the word *companion* means to break bread together. As members of the body of Christ, we are invited at Communion to gather at the Lord's table to break the bread of life together. Tonight, we will do so. We will spend the day preparing our souls and hearts.

"We begin by realizing that we were made for communion—interaction with one other and with God. We cannot be a Christian all by ourselves; fellowship is vital. Although our communities are probably flawed, in them we learn forgiveness, experience love as Christ loved, and are given opportunities to serve.

"This activity invites you to approach one another with an open heart. I will read sets of word pictures that might describe your faith journey. You will have a couple minutes to think about which description best expresses your faith journey today. Then pair off with one person in your small group and take turns reporting your choice. Provide as much detail as you are comfortable giving. Be honest, and do not judge one another.

"After a few minutes, I will read another pair of phrases. Choose which phrase best portrays your faith, or come up with your own description. This time, pair up with someone different. We will repeat this process until you've talked with everyone in the group."

Have the youth find a new partner after you ask each of these questions:

Is your faith most like . . .

→ a gentle morning sunrise, the noonday sun, or a blazing sunset lighting up the sky?

→ a Brahms' lullaby, a heavy-metal band, or a country-western song?

→ a roaring bonfire, a candle flickering in the wind, or a spotlight on a stage?

→ a seed beneath the frozen soil, a flower blooming in the spring, or a gnarly oak tree?

→ a pebble skipping over the water, or a rock rising out of the surf?

→ a gentle wind against your cheek, a tornado sweeping down, or the wind before a storm?

→ a trickle of water in a dry river bed, a swiftly flowing stream, or waves crashing on the sand?

Now have the small groups discuss these questions:

→ What did you enjoy most about this exercise? What made it difficult?

→ What did you learn about yourself?

INTERACTION EXERCISE: FAITH BLESSINGS (1 minute)

To close the first evening, invite the youth to stand in a circle and hold hands. Say: "Say to the person on your right a blessing from Paul. Say his or her name, then, 'May the grace of our Lord Jesus Christ be with your spirit.' "

SMALL-GROUP EXERCISE: BEING PRESENT (15–20 minutes)

Note: Do the individual meditations before conducting this activity.

Say: "The meditations you did earlier dealt with being present, which requires focus. One of them asked you to repeat, 'This is the day that the LORD has made; let us rejoice and be glad in it' (**Psalm 118:24**).

"When Jesus was asked what the greatest commandment is, he repeated a Scripture, known as the Shema, which was familiar to his listeners: 'You shall love the Lord your God with all your heart, and with all your soul, and with all your mind' (**Matthew 22:37**). Doing so requires a focus of love. The second part, 'Love your neighbor as yourself,' refers to what we see. Again, Jesus tells us to do something that requires focus.

"You will learn to appreciate life more fully when you practice focusing on the task or person in front of you. Being present has its own reward. It isn't easy; but with practice, you will find yourself developing this spiritual skill."

Give each group member one minute to respond to these questions:

→ How difficult or easy was it for you to practice the meditations earlier?

→ Do you think you are fairly consistent in being present, or do you often find yourself dwelling on the past or the future?

DELIBERATION EXERCISE: BEGGAR BEADS (60 minutes)

Supplies needed: Each youth will need twenty-four small beads, five larger beads, one cross bead (a small cross that can be strung on a string), and about twelve inches of string or leather

Background: Some religious traditions find prayer beads helpful. Many Protestant Christians have never tried this option. Although unfamiliar to many, prayer beads offer a means of staying focused in prayer.

The word *beggar* comes from the Middle Dutch word *begaert,* which meant "one who prays." And Saint Augustine wrote that "humans are beggars before God." So we might call prayer beads "beggar beads."

Instructions: Have the youth make beggar beads according a form developed by an Episcopal priest, Reverend Lynn Bauman, in the 1980s.

Distribute the supplies. Say: "We're going to make beggar beads. Begin by stringing your cross bead down to the middle. Then thread both strands through two larger beads. When you've gotten the string through both larger beads, separate the strands.

"Now thread seven smaller beads on each strand. You might choose colors that symbolize people or things you want to remember daily in your prayers.

For instance, a white bead might remind you of peace, or a purple bead your grandmother.

"After you string seven smaller beads, add a larger bead to each side. Continue by stringing seven more smaller beads on each side. Then thread both strands through this bead and secure with a knot. Take your time." Pause, and ask if the youth understand the pattern.

Give some background information: "Anglican Prayer Beads have thirty-three beads, which symbolize the years of Jesus' life. The cross is the focal point. The large bead after the cross is the invitatory bead; it invites you to pray. The circle also has four sets of seven beads. These sets can represent the seven days of creation, the seven days of the week, or perfection and completion, which the number seven represents in the Judeo-Christian tradition.

"Begin praying by holding the cross bead. You might try praying the Lord's Prayer with these beads, repeating it as you cover every bead. Some people pray around the circle of beads three times, an act symbolizing the triune God.

"Touch one bead at a time as you pray. Diligently touch every bead to help keep your mind from wandering. There is a rhythm to using the beads. The beads, in and of themselves, have no power; but they give you focus in prayer.

"Again, when you are making your beggar beads, you may choose special beads or colors for specific persons and concerns. When you come to that bead, remember that need in prayer. There is no right or wrong way of using this aid to prayer; find what is meaningful to you.

"A prayer known as the Jesus Prayer is, 'Lord Jesus Christ, Son of God, have mercy on me, a sinner.' People often use this prayer as a breath prayer. When breathing in, they say, 'Lord Jesus Christ, Son of God,' and while exhaling, 'have mercy on me, a sinner.'

"Bring your beggar beads to the prayer stations later on. One of the stations will provide prayer options for you to use the beads."

Ask:

➜ What is meaningful about using prayer beads?

➜ How many of you have ever tried using prayer beads?

➜ How could prayer beads deepen your prayer life?

Blessing of the Beads: Close by standing in a circle, with each person holding his or her beggar-bead necklace out in front of him or hers. Ask for volunteers to bless the use of these beads, as they help us stay focused in prayer, or repeat the following prayer:

> Lord, we know that you sanctify all of life when we offer it to you. We lift up these beads. May they remind us to pray and help us to stay focused. Thank you that your Holy Spirit carries our prayers to you and even prays for us when we are unable to pray. May prayer bring us closer to you. Bless these beads and their use. Amen.

SMALL-GROUP DISCUSSION: CELEBRATION (30 minutes)

Supplies needed: a Bible

Read **Psalm 150** and **John 15:8-11.**

Some people don't think the words *Christians* and *joy* go together. But God gives us much to celebrate and invites us to the party of life. Celebration, play, and joy really do light your soul fire.

"Joy is a result of knowing who we are: children of a Heavenly Father who created us and loves us unconditionally. Like God's love, our joy is unconditional. Our moods may fluctuate and happiness may come and go; but joy rises from a deeper place: a well of faith, hope, and love. When we abide in Christ and he lives in us, the result is joy. When we place our confidence in God's ultimate goodness, we have much to celebrate."

Tell the groups to discuss this question, allowing each member one minute to answer: Can you remember a time when you experienced joy in the midst of difficult circumstances?

Now ask, "If you haven't had that experience, have you observed people who demonstrate a deep joy even though they are facing tough times in their life?" Give each person in the group one minute to relate his or her example.

After everyone has spoken, ask:

➜ What is difference between joy and happiness?

➜ How is life different when we're in a transforming relationship with Christ?

➜ What do we have to celebrate as Christians?

CELEBRATION EXERCISE: PARTY PLANNERS
(45-60 minutes)

Supplies needed: a large roll of paper, markers, ribbon, streamers, balloons, scotch tape, masking tape or thumbtacks, dried beans and empty Easter eggs for noise makers, empty oatmeal boxes for drums, a large gift box for each small group, and wrapping paper

Preparation: Spread the supplies on a surface such as a table or floor.

Say or put in your own words: "Most Christians observe Palm Sunday, when Jesus rode into Jerusalem, fully aware of what lay ahead of him. Holy Week begins with Palm Sunday and ends with Jesus' victory over death through the Resurrection on Easter. On Palm Sunday, people laid their coats in his path and waved palm branches to herald his entry into the city. Instead of riding on a white horse, he chose a humble donkey. The people cheered.

"Who doesn't like a party? We celebrate important events. A baby is born, and an 'It's a Girl!' or 'It's a Boy!' sign is placed on the lawn. 'Graduation Party Here' signs proclaims this event. Birthdays mean noisemakers, party hats, streamers, gifts, and balloons. God calls us to celebrate that we are God's children. Another word for this celebration is *worship*. We're going to have a party to celebrate the Christian community and our source of joy: God.

"Your assignment is to help plan our worship party. I'll read off some ideas and tasks to get you started. You are not limited to these ideas; feel free to add your own."

Read aloud the following party plans:

➜ Decide what message to communicate. Make a banner and posters to hang around the room.

➜ Write a song, cheer, or poem that your small group can give as part of the celebration. You could make noisemakers or drums to enhance the music, using the supplies provided.

➜ Decide on a gift that your small group will give the group gathered here at this retreat. Decorate your gift box, and assign someone to tell about the gift.

➜ Begin to think about a gift that each of you will give God on this retreat. One of the prayer stations tonight will provide the opportunity to make a symbol of this gift.

SMALL-GROUP DISCUSSION: CONSIDERATION AND BEING KIND
(30-45 minutes)

Supplies needed: a sheet of paper and a pen or pencil for each small group

Say: "Remember a time when you performed a truly selfless act of charity or goodwill for someone. Taking the garbage out for your parents because they asked doesn't count. Each of you will be given one minute to tell your small group about your act of kindness."

After everyone has had a chance to talk, give each group a sheet of paper and a pen or pencil. Say: "As a small group, make a list of things or ideas that get in the way of acting selflessly. What prevents us from being kind and from showing consideration for others? Come up with at least twelve constraints, attitudes, or problems that thwart our kindness."

After the list making, give each person a sheet of paper and pen or pencil; ask each youth to copy his or her group's list. Next, say:

→ Cross out any obstacles that seem like ridiculous excuses.

→ Underline the most difficult barriers; narrow them down to three or fewer.

→ Put an arrow beside the things you could overcome with a little effort.

→ Put a star next to the things that would require significant work and determination to change.

→ Circle the one barrier that God would want you to surmount first.

Provide time for members of the group to relay their thoughts and choices. Ask them to name, as an act of prayer, the barrier that God would want them to surmount first. Close by praying together as a small group.

CONSIDERATION EXERCISE: CARE CARDS
(45-60 minutes)

Supplies needed: stationery-style note cards, pens, colored markers or pencils, stickers, stamps, and a stamp pad

Give each small group note cards so that it can make care cards for a specific group of people. Each member needs to make at least one card. Encourage the youth to take their time and make a nice card. They can personally sign their card and write in it, but they should also sign it, "[Name of your church] youth." You might assign recipients to each small group, such as the confirmation class, all Sunday school teachers in your church, the pastoral staff, the church administrators, and any other group you want to add.

SMALL-GROUP EXERCISE: AFFIRMATION
(15-20 minutes)

Supplies: a Bible

Read **Ephesians 4:29-32.** Say or put in your own words: "Affirmation is a gift that touches our heart, puts a smile on our face, lights our soul fire, and encourages us to be better people. But we often receive more negative than positive messages about ourselves. We need encouragement, which confirms that we matter and blesses us. We do so for other people not because they deserve it for doing something but because God is present in them.

"Christians sometimes misconstrue the message of humility and self-denial as self-depreciation. We need to remember that we are called not only to love our neighbors but also ourselves. As children of a loving Creator, Christians can rejoice and celebrate their very being and have an understanding and appreciation for self. We should place a high value on who we are and who we are called to be in Christ.

"Remember a time when someone gave you a sincere compliment or affirmed you in some other way. Each of you will be given one minute to explain the impact of this act of affirmation. How did this experience bless you?" Allow the group members to relay their experiences.

AFFIRMATION EXERCISE:
AFFIRMATION ALTERNATIVE
(30 minutes)

Supplies needed: Roles for Participants handout (on CD-ROM), a pair of scissors, and two chairs

Preparation: Print out the Roles for Participants handout, and cut out the slips as directed on the handout. Fold the slips to hide the contents.

For this exercise, your small groups need to pair up. Ask for four volunteers, and invite each of them to draw a slip of paper, which has instructions for the role they are to play. Tell the actors to keep that information private.

Ask the two actors who drew Scenario 2 to leave the room. Remind them not to disclose their instructions to each other.

Tell the rest of the group to sit in a circle. Place two chairs facing each other inside the circle. Tell the circle that its role is to carefully observe the dynamics between the players and be prepared to report what happened.

Invite the Scenario 1 actors to follow the instructions on their slips of paper. After two minutes, call time. Ask the actors to sit in the circle with the others.

Repeat the process for Scenario 2. Call time after two minutes. Invite these actors to join the circle.

Ask the youth who did not act in the scenarios to relate what they observed.

Next, have the speaking actors speak about how they felt as they tried to describe their experiences and opinions.

Ask the silent actors to reveal their instructions and talk about how easy or difficult this exercise was for them.

Open the discussion to the whole group, asking:

→ What differences did you observe between the two scenarios?

→ What conclusions might you make, now that you know the actors' roles?

→ How does listening intently become a blessing of affirmation to someone?

CLOSING WORSHIP
(60 minutes)

Supplies needed: Prayer Stations handout (on CD-ROM) and the supplies listed on the handout

Preparation: Spread the tables or storage bins around the area, cover them with cloth, and put a candle and one of the prayer-station cut-outs on them.

Have a time of singing; then tell the youth they can pray at their own pace around any of the stations.

Faith Prints

Focus: to discover the ways in which God leaves "prints" for us to follow

Key Scripture: "Faith is the substance of things hoped for, the evidence of things not seen" (Hebrews 11:1, KJV).

Organize the retreat options to fit your schedule, but do the Faith Prints worship service (on CD-ROM) the first thing on the first night.

Options

→ First-Evening Activity 1: Making Mailboxes

→ First-Evening Activity 2: Walking by Faith

→ Small-Group Session 1: Faith Steps—Beginning the Journey (three activities)

→ Small-Group Session 2: Bible Study on the Good Samaritan

→ Small-Group Session 3: God-Prints Photo Shoot

→ Small-Group Session 4: Faith-Print Mentors

→ Large-Group Session 1: Faith-Print-Possibility Posters

→ Large-Group Session 2: Discovering God Prints

→ Large-Group Session 3: Creative Prints

→ Large-Group Movie Clips

Reproducible Handouts (on CD-ROM)

→ Faith Prints worship service with "Faith Prints" skit (on CD-ROM), from *Worship Feast: Services—50 Complete Multisensory Services for Youth*

→ God Prints

→ Saturday-Morning Individual Meditation

→ Sunday-Morning Individual Meditation

FIRST-EVENING ACTIVITY 1: MAKING MAILBOXES
(60 minutes)

Supplies: scissors, markers, paper, pens, glue, a maps, a footprint stamp, and ink pads. You will also need a shoe box or cake-mix box for each youth on your retreat.

Give each adult leader a list of names for his or her small group so the leader can confirm who is in his or her group.

Invite each youth and adult leader to decorate his or her mailbox. (See page 11.) Encourage the students to decorate their mailboxes with maps, footprints, and fingerprints. Provide footprint cut-outs, extra map pieces, a footprint stamp, and ink pads.

FIRST-EVENING ACTIVITY 2: WALKING BY FAITH
(60 minutes)

Supplies: a blindfold, some candles, matches, and a long line of rope for each small group

The faith walk is done in small groups. Lead the session outdoors if you can; it works best on a dark night.

Give each small group a rope. Each small group's adult leader should tell the members to blindfold themselves then to hold on to the rope. The leader should slowly take the group on a walk, giving instructions to be passed down the line, such as, "We are approaching a tree; touch the tree as we slowly walk around it." Remind the groups to move slowly.

Allow at least twenty minutes for the walk. Give a signal to end this activity.

When the small groups return from their walks, have them remain blindfolded and ask them to stand quietly holding hands while you read the following Scripture: "For we walk by faith, not by sight" (**2 Corinthians 5:7**).

Say: "Sometimes, walking by faith feels a lot like walking blindfolded or in the dark. Doing so requires trust. Having someone leading you and looking out for your well-being helps immensely, as does traveling with others on this faith journey. But you won't get anywhere if you don't take that first step and keep walking. Christ invites you to walk in the light—the newness of the life in him."

Have the youth remove their blindfolds, and light some of the candles.

Gather the group together (or have the youth remain in small groups) to discuss some questions by candle light:

→ How would you describe this experience?

→ What made the walk difficult?

→ How easy was it to trust the person in front of you?

→ Did anything distract you from this activity?

→ What helped you walk together?

SMALL-GROUP SESSION 1: FAITH STEPS—BEGINNING THE JOURNEY (45-60 minutes)

Supplies: magazines, newspapers, markers, posterboard, glue, scissors, one Bible per small group, and masking tape or thumbtacks

Part 1: Have the students begin by reading Hebrews 11:1 in their small groups. Next, give each group markers and a posterboard. Have the groups make "What is Faith?" graffiti boards by brainstorming things they believe in but have never seen and by writing these things on its posterboard.

When the groups are finished, they should discuss the following questions:

→ What helps us believe in things we have never seen?

→ What makes it difficult to believe in things we have never seen?

Part 2: Now distribute the magazines, newspapers, scissors, and glue. Have the groups use the posterboard from the last activity to make a group collage of ideas, products, and things we are asked to "believe in" or "have faith" in. Examples include pills that help you loose forty pounds, ointment that helps bald people grow hair, greeting cards that will improve your relationships with others, and other promises from the government or the science community.

Then ask the groups:

→ What means are used to get us to believe in something?

→ Are some things easier to believe in than others? Why?

→ What helps convince you to have faith in a product, organization, or idea?

→ What does it mean to believe in something?

Part 3: This activity requires the group to look at a few specific areas of their lives to see what kind of convictions they have. Some of the categories are light and fun; others are serious. Ask the small groups to go around their circle, with everyone completing each of these sentences after you read it:

→ One thing I'm convinced about food is . . .

→ One thing I'm convinced about money is . . .

→ One thing I'm convinced about exercise is . . .

→ One thing I'm convinced about the circus is . . .

→ One thing I'm convinced about my parents is . . .

→ One thing I'm convinced about myself is . . .

→ One thing I'm convinced about God is . . .

→ One thing I'm convinced about my faith is . . .

Next, have the groups discuss the following questions, allowing some time for discussion between the questions:

→ Why, do you think, were some sentences easier to complete than others?

→ Was there one particular sentence that was the most difficult for you to complete? If so, which one, and why?

→ What insight have you gained from this activity?

Come back together as a whole group. Allow each small group to talk for a while about its collage. Affix the collages onto your worship center or altar for the weekend.

SMALL-GROUP SESSION 2: BIBLE STUDY ON THE GOOD SAMARITAN (45 minutes)

Supplies needed: a Bible and a Bible paraphrase such as *The Message* (optional)

Before you read the Scripture, ask the whole group what it remembers about the story of the good Samaritan. Ask where it took place, who was involved, and what the youth remember about the characters in the story. What do they know about the relationship between the Samaritans and the Jews?

Now read the parable of the good Samaritan (**Luke 10:25-37**) to the small groups. If you have time, use two versions, including a paraphrase.

Have the groups discuss the following questions, leaving time in between questions for discussion:

→ Whom did you find yourself relating to in the story?

→ Who was the person asking Jesus the questions the first part of the passage?

→ What could be some of the reasons the lawyer asked Jesus the two questions?

→ How did the expert in the Law regard the Samaritan?

→ What was Jesus trying to communicate to the expert in the Law?

If the youth don't comprehend Jesus' message, explain that Jesus was saying that it is not OK just to understand what you should do and that you should also act on your faith; you need to leave some faith prints.

→ How does the expert in the law answer Jesus' question "Which of these three, do you think, was a neighbor?" (**Luke 10:36b**)? Why, do you think, did the expert answer the way he did?

Inform the group that the expert could not identify with the Samaritan, because doing so was far out of his cultural reach. He could not even say the word *Samaritan* but only "the one who showed him mercy."

→ Can you remember a time when you related more to the expert in the Law than to the good Samaritan?

To spark conversation, think of an example or a possible situation where a young person might have difficulty acting on his or her faith.

→ Can you think of a circumstance where we have been required to think of faith or ideas that are outside our cultural reach?

Have the groups wrap up their discussion by talking about ways in which this story challenges them. Lastly, ask the youth to pray in their small groups.

SMALL-GROUP SESSION 3:
GOD-PRINTS PHOTO SHOOT
(60 minutes)

Supplies: a disposable, instant, or digital camera for each small group; and a printer (optional)

Say or put in your own words: "God speaks to us through creation, other people, and the Holy Spirit. God is revealed though all of life, and we need to look for the signs of God's prints.

"Each small group will be given a camera. Your assignment is to take photos of God prints. You may recall something in nature that you observed this morning during your meditation time. Allow each person in your small group to take at least one photo. Your group can pose in various ways to symbolize how you experience God prints in other people. Use your imaginations, and tune in to God's presence. Return the cameras to the leader at the end of this session."

For disposable cameras, take them to a one-hour development center; for digital cameras, use a printer. Make the photos available for your final worship service.

SMALL-GROUP SESSION 4:
FAITH-PRINT MENTORS
(45-60 minutes)

Supplies: several markers and a sheet of newsprint or large sheet of paper for each person, and an extra sheet for each small group

Give each person a sheet and some markers. Instruct the youth to make a timeline of their life (birth to their current age). Ask them to draw or write down, next to the corresponding years, who has left faith prints on their life. Encourage the students to think of all the people who have nurtured the seeds of faith. Who are the people who taught them, prayed for them, and extended other acts of love and kindness to them?

When the youth are finished, invite them to talk about the timelines. Ask them to mention traits these persons demonstrated.

Give each small group another sheet. Conclude by having each group compile a list of actions as a means of leaving faith prints, as well as the people for whom they hope to leave faith prints.

LARGE-GROUP SESSION 1: FAITH-PRINT-POSSIBILITY POSTERS
(45 minutes)

Supplies needed: Faith-Print-Possibility posters (on CD-ROM)

Preparation: Around the room, hang each of the posters, which describe ways to leave faith prints.

Say or put in your own words: "Faith is not something we just talk about or experience. It changes our behavior and our way of thinking."

Invite the youth to walk around the room and read each of the statements. They should note which of these actions they would find easy to do and which would be highly uncomfortable for them. There are no right or wrong answers; each person will respond differently. Give the students five to ten minutes to read all the statements.

Say, "Choose one example that you would feel most comfortable doing, and sit below that poster." After the youth are situated, say: "For ten minutes, in these groups, relate an instance when you have done what the statement says or why you could easily do so." If there is a lone student at a poster, ask him or her to move to the closest youth for discussion. If there are ten or more teens at one poster, ask them to break into two or more small groups.

After discussion, say: "Now choose one example that you would feel highly uncomfortable doing. For ten minutes discuss with the other youth under the same poster why you would find this activity difficult."

After discussion, say: "Choose one poster that states something you would like to do or that you feel would stretch you and help you grow in faith. For ten minutes, talk in these groups."

LARGE-GROUP SESSION 2: DISCOVERING GOD PRINTS
(30 minutes)

Supplies needed: copies of God Prints handout (on CD-ROM)

Say or put in your own words: "As the source of life and the foundation of our being, God is active in our lives all the time. God speaks to us through creation, other people, and the Holy Spirit. God is revealed in all of life—we just need to look for the signs.

"Begin to focus on God's prints, which are all around. Where do you find the evidence of God? Someone once said, 'Wherever there is love, creativity, healing, peace, wisdom or justice, there is the power of God.' "

"To help you become more aware of the God prints around you, find someone you don't know very well to be your partner. Together you will complete a handout I will give you. You are to look at the picture and guess what evidence of God's love and care for us is in the picture."

The answers may include: 1) your inner being or soul; 2) through reading the Bible or other books of wisdom; 3) nature and God's creation; 4) prayer; 5) music and the arts; 6) Jesus Christ; 7) other people; 8) voices; 9) signs that provide direction; 10) stillness and solitude. The youth may come up with other interpretations; there are no predetermined "correct" answers for this exercise.

When the youth are finished, ask each pair to join with two other pairs. Have these groups of six explain their responses.

LARGE-GROUP SESSION 3: CREATIVE PRINTS
(45 minutes)

Supplies: polymer clay of various colors, hemp or leather for necklaces, sculpting tools, an oven, and paper towels and water for cleanup

Invite each person to create a small symbol of a God print or faith print by using the clay. Tell the youth these symbols will be baked and then strung for necklaces. Remind them to make a hole at the top for stringing.

LARGE-GROUP MOVIE CLIP 1: FAITH STEPS, BABY STEPS
(45 minutes)

Supplies: a DVD player or VHS player, a TV, and the movie *What About Bob?*

Preparation: Obtain a video- or DVD-viewing license if you need to. (See page 2.) If using a VHS, fast forward it to 11:24:00 minutes.

As a group, watch the clip from *What About Bob?* when Bob leaves his therapist's office, having been told to take "baby steps." Bob is trying to get on the elevator. (VHS stop time is 15:31:00.)

Say: "Bob's fears prevent him for even getting on an elevator. His anxiety makes life difficult for him." Have the youth discuss in their small groups the following questions:

➜ What anxieties do you think people have about making a faith commitment?

➜ What makes having faith difficult?

Say: "Sometimes we think that to become spiritual is an unreachable goal. We don't even try because it seems too difficult.

"Bob is told to begin with baby steps. As a group, come up with a list identifying baby steps that could help someone grow in his or her faith journey. At the end of this session, all of the small groups will meet together to present their suggestions." Allow the youth to make their lists. After a few minutes, gather the groups and have them read aloud their lists.

LARGE-GROUP MOVIE-CLIP 2:
FAITH STEPS—TIME TO CHOOSE
(45 minutes)

Note: This activity is suggested for the second night of a two-night retreat. The follow-up questions can be done in small groups or as a large group.

Supplies needed: a DVD or VHS player, a TV, and the movie *The Legend of Bagger Vance*

Preparation: Obtain a video- or DVD-viewing license if you need to. (See page 2 for details.)

Show the scene where Junuh says, "I can't do this" (VHS time: 1:38:32–1:42:30; DVD Chapter 17.) Then ask these follow-up questions:

→ Junuh says, "I can't do this." What was he feeling?

→ What makes you feel like you "can't do this"?

→ Bagger Vance mentions "a game can't be won, only played." What do you think he means?

→ Vance goes on to say, "Time to go on, lay it down. You got a choice. You can stop or start ...walkin'.... Time for you to choose." Have you ever felt God saying those same words to you? What do you think Vance means by "time to choose"? by "stop or start"?

→ Junuh says, "I can't." Vance responds, "Yes, you can. You ain't alone. I'm right here with ya. I've been here all along. And play the game. The game that only you is made to play. You were given this game when you came into this world." Imagine God saying those same words to you. How would you respond to God asking you to play the game or to live the life only you were made to live?

Soul Mates: Friends for the Journey

Focus: to grow together as a community and as disciples of Christ

Key Scripture: "Love one another with mutual affection; outdo one another in showing honor" (Romans 12:10).

Organize the retreat options to fit your schedule, doing the Large-Group Gathering Session first, Family Feud toward the end of the retreat, and the Closing Worship last. A flier for the Closing Worship is on the CD-ROM.

Options
→ Large-Group Gathering Session: Fellowship and Friendship
→ Small-Group Activity 1: What We Expect
→ Small-Group Activity 2: What God Expects
→ Small-Group Activity 3: Creating a Fellowship Poster
→ Large-Group Activity 1: Living in Harmony
→ Large-Group Activity 2: Stealing Laundry
→ Small-Group Activity 4: Forgive One Another
→ Large-Group Activity 3: Make Party Hats
→ Large-Group Activity 4: Family Feud

Reproducible Handouts (on CD-ROM)
→ Good-Friends Survey
→ Living-in-Harmony Prep Sheet
→ Forgive One Another
→ Family Feud
→ Closing-Worship Bulletin

LARGE-GROUP GATHERING SESSION: FELLOWSHIP AND FRIENDSHIP
(10 minutes)

Supplies needed: Bibles

Ask for volunteers to read **John 15:12, Romans 12:10,** and **Galatians 5:13.**

Say or put in your own words: "Christians are to love one another and to experience what the Bible calls fellowship. Over the course of this retreat, Soul Mates: Friends for the Journey, we are going to look at various aspects of fellowship, which is a lot like friendship."

SMALL-GROUP ACTIVITY 1: WHAT WE EXPECT
(60 minutes)

Supplies needed: a pen and a Good-Friends Survey (on CD-ROM) per youth

Hand out a pen and a survey to each youth, and say: "Put a check mark beside each statement you think is true. Do so as quickly as possible, going with your first reaction." Give the small groups time to complete the survey.

When the youth are finished, say: "Your small-group members will now take turns reading a statement out loud to your group. When a statement is read, raise your hand if you checked it. If everyone in your group raises his or her hand, circle the statement. If no one raises a hand, draw a line through the statement. If only some of your group members raise their hands, write down how many did so and how many did not. At this point, do not discuss the statements; just go through the list."

When the groups are finished, have them discuss these questions:

→ How easy or difficult was this exercise for you? Why?

→ Have someone read the statements your group totally agreed on. Why are these qualities important for a good friendship? What good qualities would you add to this list?

→ Now have someone read the statements that no one in your group checked. What can we learn from this list? What would you add?

Now ask the groups to read the statements on which they disagreed. For each of these sentences, have the youth discuss the question,

➜ Why did or didn't you check this statement?

Ask the youth to give equal time to both opinions.

When conversation is dying down, ask if anyone in any of the groups would like to change his or her opinion about a statement. The objective is not for everyone to agree but for everyone to think and feel free to challenge. Point out that it is OK to disagree in a healthy relationship.

Remind the groups that over the course of the retreat, they're going to learn what it means to be good friends on the Christian journey.

SMALL-GROUP ACTIVITY 2: WHAT GOD EXPECTS
(20 minutes)

Supplies needed: plain paper, pens, at least one large sheet of paper (such as newsprint), markers, thumbtacks or masking tape, Bibles, and Bible paraphrases such as *The Message* or the *The Living Bible*

Preparation: Write the following Scripture references on one or more large sheets of paper: **John 15:12; Romans 12:10; Galatians 5:13; 1 John 4:16.**

Say: "In the twelfth century, a monk named Aelred (AYL-red) of Rievaulx (ree-VOH) did a lot of thinking and writing about friendship. He thought that a good paraphrase of **1 John 4:16** was 'God is friendship.'"

Ask the small groups to divide into partners; then distribute a Bible, pen, and sheet of paper to each pair. Hold up the sheet of Scripture references, and say: "I want you and your partner to paraphrase these Scriptures. A paraphrase is simply a way of interpreting Scripture and putting it in your own words. If you have difficulty writing a paraphrase, you may read the verse from one of the Bible paraphrases to get some ideas."

After three to five minutes, have each pair read aloud the original Scripture and their paraphrase to the others in their small groups. Then give the pairs masking tape or thumbtacks so that they can post their paraphrases around the room.

SMALL-GROUP ACTIVITY 3:
CREATING A FELLOWSHIP POSTER
(30-40 minutes)

Supplies needed: Bibles, paper, pens, posterboard, magazines, scissors, glue, markers, and thumbtacks or masking tape

Have the small groups discuss the question, What does God expect of us in our relationships with others?

Next, distribute a Bible, pen, and sheet of paper to each group. Tell the groups to read **Romans 12:9-21** and make a list of the qualities for Christian fellowship that are based on this Scripture.

After a few minutes, distribute posterboard, magazines, scissors, glue, and markers. Invite each group to create a poster that conveys the group's findings from the Scripture passage. When the students are finished, give them thumbtacks or tape, and ask them to hang the posters around the room.

LARGE-GROUP SESSION 1:
LIVING IN HARMONY WITH ONE ANOTHER
(90 minutes–2 hours)

Note: This activity is intended for nine or more youth and four adult leaders.

Supplies needed: Living-in-Harmony Prep Sheet (on CD-ROM), Bibles, one deck of playing cards per twenty-one youth (with each deck displaying a different back), markers, construction paper, and two large sheets of paper

Preparation: Prepare each deck according to the instructions on Living-in-Harmony Prep Sheet. Inform several adult leaders about their role in the game.

Game time: Ask several youth to read aloud **Romans 12:15-16; 1 Corinthians 12:20, 26;** and **Colossians 3:14.**

Read aloud or put in your own words: "We are called to be in community, or fellowship, with others. We know that God wants us to love and forgive one another. But God also wants us to laugh and cry together—to celebrate and rejoice when good things happen to others and share in one another's pain and sorrows. Doing so is the opposite of jealousy and envy."

Have each youth randomly select a card from the deck.

All students who drew a club should gather and find a meeting space. The adult worker with this group should say: "Think about your individual interests and traits. With the markers and construction paper provided, create your personal shield that represents your unique characteristics, interests, and skills. The shield should tell a little about who you are. You will have fifteen to twenty minutes for this task."

All students who drew a spade should gather together and find a meeting space. The adult volunteer meeting with this group should ask each of these students to pair off with someone.

Next, the leader should say: "With your partner, find out what characteristics you two share, or what makes you distinct as a pair. With the construction paper and markers provided, create a family shield together that represents all of the traits you've found the two of you share. You will have fifteen to twenty minutes for this task."

All students who drew a heart should gather and find a meeting space. If you have prepared more than one deck of cards, the adult working with this group should say, "There are different heart groups; match the back of your card to find your group."

After the regrouping, the adult should say: "After I read the instructions, your group should choose a leader to facilitate the tasks I'm about to describe.

"As a group, you will come up with a set of characteristics that make your group distinct and that everyone in your group shares. It may have something to do with clothing, the music you listen to, the sports you play, or what you eat for breakfast.

"You also need to create rules that someone must follow in order to join your group. Some of your rules may be secret, such as, 'To be a part of this group, you must salute the leader with your left hand.'

"On a large sheet of paper, create your tribal shield that represents your set of characteristics and your rules. You will have fifteen to twenty minutes for this task."

All students who drew a diamond should gather and find a meeting place. If you have prepared more than one deck of cards, the adult working with this group should say, "There are different diamond groups; match the back of your card to find your group."

After the regrouping, the adult should say: "After I read the instructions, your group should choose a leader to facilitate the tasks I'm about to describe.

"As a group, you will come up with a set of characteristics that make your group distinct and that everyone in your group shares. It may have something to do with clothing, the music you listen to, the sports you play, or what you eat for breakfast.

"You also need to create rules that someone must follow in order to join your group. Some of your rules may be secret, such as, 'To be a part of this group, you must salute the leader with your left hand.'

"On a large sheet of paper, create a shield that represents your characteristics and your rules. You will have fifteen to twenty minutes for this task."

Tell all of the diamond and heart groups to stay together and not to mix with any of the other heart or diamond groups.

After all of the youth have finished their creations, go over to the students who drew clubs, and tell them: "When I tell you to, I want you to visit the heart and diamond groups. You'll have five minutes to find a heart or diamond group to fit into. However, you must meet a group's requirements to join it. If you can't find a group to join, you must remain alone." Have the clubs wait for their cue.

Next, go over to the spades and say to them: "When I tell you to, I want you to visit the heart and diamond groups. You'll have five minutes to determine if your pair could fit in with one of the heart or diamond groups. However, you must meet a group's requirements to join it. If you cannot fit in with a large group, you must remain a pair." Have the spades to wait for their cue.

For the first round: Bring only a few of the clubs and spades back. Don't instruct the hearts and diamonds to do anything to recruit members.

For the second round: This time, ask the diamonds and hearts to actively recruit members, doing all they can to find new members. Then bring in the remaining spades and clubs.

After the rounds, ask for reports and discussion:

➜ (To the spades) Tell us about your experiences of determining which crowd to join. Where did you end up, and why?

➜ (To the clubs) Tell us about your experience.

RETREATS & LOCK-INS

→ (To the diamonds and hearts) Describe the rules and regulations of your group.

→ How was this experience similar to real life? How was it different?

→ What groups at school remind you of the hearts and diamonds?

→ Who reminds you of the spades?

→ Who reminds you of the clubs?

→ What insights does the activity give you about school or life in general? What are you thinking??

LARGE-GROUP ACTIVITY 2: STEALING LAUNDRY
(45 minutes)

Supplies needed: four or five clothespins for each person, cones to mark the boundaries for the game, a whistle, and enough boxes of snack bars so that every participant can have one bar

Give each person four or five clothespins. Instruct the youth to clip them on the back of their shirts. Point out the boundaries.

Say: "The object of the game is to collect as many clothespins as you can. Once all your clothespins have been removed from your back, you can no longer 'steal' clothespins from others and you must stand on the edge of the boundary. If you remove the last clothespin from someone, tell him or her that he or she is now out of the game.

"You may remove only one clothespin from each individual; you may not take more than one clothespin from the same person. A whistle will start and stop the game. You may not hit, tackle, or engage in other violent behavior; but you may run."

Blow the whistle to start and to end the game. The time necessary depends on the size of your group. After the game is finished, determine the top six winners and give each of them a box of snack bars. These youth will have enough for the entire group if they share.

SMALL-GROUP ACTIVITY 4: FORGIVE ONE ANOTHER
(60 minutes)

Supplies needed: copies of the Forgive One Another handout (on CD-ROM), pens, and Bibles

Spend some time discussing the stealing-laundry game. Ask:

→ Was anyone from our small group a winner?

→ Was anyone eliminated fairly quickly? If so, how do you feel?

→ How many of you felt you spent more effort defending your clothespins than trying to steal others? Did this strategy work?

→ How did it feel to play a game in which the only way to win was to take from others?

Say: "That game was a fun attempt to introduce our next theme, Forgive One Another. As Christians, we are called to do something that is unnatural for most humans: to forgive others for wrongs against us. Let's look at what Scripture tells us about forgiveness and then figure out why we need to forgive to have community, keep fellowship, and find soul mates."

Distribute the out the Forgive One Another Handouts. Have some volunteers read the printed Scriptures.

Next, tell the youth to write about an incident for which they need forgiveness. Ask them to complete the thought *I ask forgiveness for . . .* on their handout. Tell the students not to use real names or give too many details, since other youth will read the sheets.

Now ask the teens to think of someone or something they need to forgive. Tell them to write it on their handout but not to use someone's real name.

Say: "Perhaps the person has asked you for forgiveness or said he or she was sorry; maybe not. You still need to forgive the person." Allow a few minutes for the youth to complete their writing.

Have the youth tear off the top half of the paper that has the forgiveness statements and turn them in to you. Shuffle the slips, and redistribute them.

Ask the youth to each read aloud the statement they have. Do not allow anyone to comment on an incident.

Next, have the groups discuss these questions (which are on the handout):

➜ Is it easier to forgive, or to request forgiveness? Why?

➜ Are some things easier to forgive than others? If so, why?

➜ Who is hurt the most if you refuse to forgive?

➜ What are the results of not forgiving?

➜ What does forgiveness mean?

➜ What are the benefits of forgiving others?

➜ Is there anything God will not forgive?

➜ How do we experience God's forgiveness?

Collect all the cards after the discussion.

Join hands, and pray, focusing on forgiveness. You can do so however you feel comfortable: by leading the prayer, by having each youth say a brief prayer or ask for forgiveness, or by saying the Lord's Prayer together.

LARGE-GROUP ACTIVITY 3: MAKE PARTY HATS (60 minutes)

Supplies needed: scissors, markers, glue, construction paper, silk flowers, ribbon, stickers, tissue paper, balloons, feathers, and sewing trims such as rickrack and pompoms. (This activity is a good way to recycle odd materials!)

Celebrate one another by making party hats that reflect individual personalities, interests, special gifts, and talents.

Ask that the youth write on their hat any achievements or honors they have received. They should include their good traits, such as what they like about themselves and what others like about them. Give the youth about thirty minutes to make their hats.

Ask the youth to tell their small groups about what is on their hats. When the teens are finished describing their hats, have them give their hat to the person on their right. Tell the youth that when they are given someone else's hat, they should put it on; this act symbolizes that we rejoice with one another and celebrate the other person's gifts, abilities, and accomplishments.

Close by having each group stand in a circle and hold hands while you read this blessing: "May we be united in the fellowship of Jesus Christ. Let us laugh together and cry together. Teach us how to love one another. Forgive us, and prod us to forgive one another. May this retreat be an experience in which we celebrate one another. Let us be soul mates in you. Amen."

Tell the groups to leave their hats on for the Family Feud game.

LARGE GROUP ACTIVITY 4: FAMILY FEUD

Supplies needed: Family Feud surveys (on CD-ROM)

Preparation: Some time during the retreat, have one of your adult volunteers distribute the Family Feud survey and get answers from as many youth as possible. He or she should keep track of how many people were surveyed. When the youth have turned in a good number of surveys, the leader should tally the number of like answers to each question. (For instance, in response to "Name your favorite fruit," twenty people may have written, "bananas"; sixteen people, "apples"; and one person, "pomegranate.")

Game time: To begin the game, divide the groups into two teams and have the teams create a family name. Each team will send one person to answer the first question of each round. Read the two youth a statement from the survey, and ask them to guess the most popular answer to that statement. Whichever person guesses the more popular answer first gets to decide if his or her team will play or pass to the next team.

If the student chooses to play, one of his or her team members has to guess another answer to the same statement. If that team member guesses an answer that made the surveyed list, the team gets a point; if not, he or she gets a strike. If two other team members each get a strike, the opposing team gets one guess at the same category's answer. If the opposing team answers correctly, they get the point for that round; if not, the first team gets the point.

Play as many rounds as desired or until a certain number of points is reached.

Hope: the Rock

Focus: to help youth put their hope in God alone

Key Scripture: "May the God of hope fill you with all joy and peace as you trust in [God], so that you may overflow with hope by the power of the Holy Spirit" (Romans 15:13, NIV).

Options

→ Large-Group Gathering Session

→ Small-Group Activity 1: Hope in God

→ Small-Group Activity 2: Foundation Blocks

→ Small-Group Activity 3: Foundation Rocks

Reproducible Handouts (on CD-ROM)

→ First-Morning Individual Meditation

→ Second-Morning Individual Meditation

→ Foundation Rocks

LARGE-GROUP GATHERING SESSION
(10 minutes)

Ask the group to join you in an opening prayer. Use your own words, or pray: "God, our rock, the foundation of our lives: Be with each person in our group this morning. Help us to open our hearts and tune in to your spirit so we may learn eternal truths. Thank you for being the rock that holds us when all else seems to give way. Amen."

Read aloud or put in your own words: "Hope is pretty important. **Hebrews 6:19** describes it as an anchor for the soul. Other verses refer to God as the rock of hope. Everyone needs hope to survive. Feeling that life is hopeless can cause depression and lead to all kinds of destructive behavior, not only to ourselves but also to others. It can create an attitude that nothing matters."

SMALL-GROUP ACTIVITY 1:
HOPE IN GOD
(60 minutes)

Supplies needed: several magazines for each small group

Ask, "How would you describe feelings of hopelessness?" Have the groups make a list of descriptions of hopelessness. Then ask, "What are some examples of behavior that indicate someone feels life is hopeless?"

Read aloud or put in your own words: "Even infants need hope. The foundation for their identity and hope for life comes from their caretakers. Somewhere in the human psyche is a need for hope.

"This session looks at hope, which, in the Bible, is essential and endures forever. If hope is so important, we need to look at what gives us hope. On what do we base our hope?"

Have the groups look through the magazines and find examples of where the media and advertisers tell you to base hope. (If the youth are bewildered, give them a couple of the following examples: popularity, having the right things, science, military might, the government, money, and investments.)

Give each group time to find examples from magazines and to explain what the examples offer. Have the group identify which of its examples would be an unwise basis for hope.

Ask:

→ Which of these examples would be good places to put your hope in?

→ How do we as a society place our hope in these things?

→ When have you put your hope in one of these things? What was the result?

Read **Matthew 7:24-29.** Ask, "What does the Scripture we just read have to do with the activity we just did?"

Say: "Hope that is solid and worth building your life upon is based on God. In both the Old and New Testaments, the translations for the word *hope* are always linked with trust in God."

SMALL-GROUP ACTIVITY 2: FOUNDATION BLOCKS
(60 minutes)

Supplies needed: paper, a pen or pencil, an envelope, a pair of scissors (optional), a marker or piece of chalk, and a large writing surface

Preparation: Cut or tear the paper into strips, and write on each strip one of the following "foundation blocks": *prayer, friends and mentors, good health, basic needs are met, a future to look forward to, final triumph of good over evil, loving and forgiving nature of God, love and nurture of family, the promises of God*

Say: "Now we're going to do an exercise that will remind us of where to find hope and evaluate the basis for our hope. Since ancient times, Christianity has offered solid ground on which to place our trust. Throughout the ages, including times of persecution and famine, Christians have held to these foundation blocks and found God to be unfailing."

Have one person at a time come forward and draw a slip of paper. Tell each youth to to act out for his or her small group the foundation block written on the slip. The students should act out in a charades style. (If the youth need a reminder of how to play charades, give them a refresher course on the rules.)

If the small group can't guess the correct answer within a minute, have the person read what his or her paper says. Next, have the actor tell why this foundation block is important for hope. When the person is done, ask the group for comments, additions, or questions.

Take turns until each foundation block has been read.

When everyone has finished talking about the foundation blocks, write each of those words or phrases on a large writing surface. Ask your students to rank them, beginning with the easiest to lose and still have hope, and ending with the most difficult to lose and still have hope. (This activity should stimulate some interesting and lively discussion as the group attempts to prioritize these elements of hope.)

Ask the youth to explain their rankings by giving examples. You might ask:

→ Are there people in this world who have little food and still have faith?

→ Why is it more difficult to have hope when basic needs are not met?

→ Are there people who are dying and still have a sense of hope?

→ Can you think of people who have been isolated from friends of family but haven't given up hope?"

SMALL-GROUP ACTIVITY 3: FOUNDATION ROCKS
(60 minutes)

Supplies needed: pens and a copy of Foundation Rocks handout (on CD-ROM) for each youth

Distribute the Foundation Rocks handouts. Have your group spend a few minutes thinking about where they put their trust and hope. Give about five minutes for this introspective experience.

Use the handout as a basis for each youth to make observations on these various areas of their lives. Ask them to rate the areas as to how much difficulty or ease they have in putting their trust in an area. Invite the youth also to make notes of times when they have experienced hope because of one of the "rocks," or foundations.

Bring the groups back together, and ask:

→ What did you learn about yourself from this exercise?

→ What was easy to write about or ponder?

→ What was difficult?

→ Why were some things easier to write and think about than others?

→ What one "rock" would help you have a stronger sense of hope would you like to strengthen?

Have all of the groups join hands in a prayer circle. Close the session by reading **Romans 15:13** as a prayer for your group: "May the God of hope fill you with all joy and peace as you trust in him, so that you may overflow with hope by the power of the Holy Spirit" (NIV).

Ready to Go → Christmas Retreat

Focus: to help youth participate in the Christmas story and affirm their belief in Christ

Key Scripture: "When the angels had left them and gone into heaven, the shepherds said to one another, 'Let us go now to Bethlehem and see this thing that has taken place, which the Lord has made known to us'" (Luke 2:15).

Options

→ Large-Group Opening Activity: Sing We All of Christmas

→ Small-Group Activity: Christmas Expectations

→ Small-Group Activity: Living the Story

→ Large-Group Activity: Revealing Your Group's Identity

→ Closing Experience: Who Do You Say That I Am?

Reproducible Handouts (on CD-ROM)

→ Group 1

→ Group 2

→ Group 3

→ Group 4

→ Group 5

→ Choral Reading

LARGE-GROUP OPENING ACTIVITY: SING WE ALL OF CHRISTMAS
(15 minutes)

Supplies needed: paper, a pen or pencil, and a pair or scissors (optional)

Preparation: Cut or tear the paper into slips, with one slip per youth. Write the name of each youth on the one of a slip.

Then organize the names into the small groups you have assigned. On the back of each group's slips, write one of these Christmas-carol titles: "Joy to the World," "Hark! the Herald Angels Sing," "Silent Night," "O Come, All Ye Faithful," and "Away in a Manger." Each group should have a different title written on the back of its slips.

At gathering time, give each student the slip with his or her name on it. Tell the youth that when you say, "Go," they are to start singing the carol on their paper and find their small group. Address any questions; then say, "Go."

SMALL-GROUP ACTIVITY: CHRISTMAS EXPECTATIONS
(60–90 minutes)

Preparation: If you need to, obtain a movie-viewing license. (See page 2.)

Supplies needed: a large writing surface, a marker or piece of chalk, a small prize for each group (such as candy canes or nuts), paper, pens or pencils, and a video tape or DVD of *A Christmas Story*

Say: "Your small group will work together to answer some questions about the Christmas story. The first group to have a member silently raise his or her hand gets the first shot at answering each question. If the first team answers incorrectly, another team will get to answer, and then another, until a team gets it right. When a team answers correctly, it will get one point. The team with the most correct answers will get a prize. Ready?"

When the youth are ready, ask them these questions:

→ Where was Mary and Joseph's hometown? (Nazareth)

→ Who was the angel that appeared to Mary? (Gabriel)

➜ To what other individuals did an angel appear? (Zechariah and Joseph)

➜ Who was Mary's cousin who was also with child? (Elizabeth)

➜ What does *Emmanuel* mean? (God with us)

➜ Who was the King of Judea at the time of Jesus' birth? (Herod)

➜ Why did Jesus' parents have to go to Bethlehem? (to register for the census)

➜ Why did Mary give birth in a stable? (no room at the inn)

➜ Who were the first people to visit the baby Jesus? (shepherds)

➜ How did the shepherd know about the birth of Jesus? (angel chorus)

Ask the groups to discuss the expectations they or people in general have at Christmastime. When the youth have talked for a few minutes, ask for the groups to relay to the whole group a few expectations they mentioned.

Now show the scene from *A Christmas Story* where Ralphie has a cowboy fantasy (VHS time: 21:48:00–24:00:00; DVD Chapter 8). Stop at the point where his dad enters the kitchen. Ask:

➜ How many of you can relate to this story?

➜ What did you want more than anything when you were a little kid?

➜ Can you recall a particular Christmas when you just had to have something?

Distribute paper and writing utensils, and have everyone write a list of things they want or need this Christmas. Then ask the youth to evaluate which things are wants and which are needs and to put a star next to the needs.

Read Isaiah 2:1-5; 9:2-7; 40:1-5. Ask:

➜ What did Ralphie want more than anything for Christmas?

➜ Why, do you think, did he want the BB gun?

➜ In what ways were his expectations unrealistic?

➜ When did you have unrealistic expectations for Christmas?

Say, "At the time of Jesus' birth, the Jews had been waiting for hundreds of years for a messiah." Read **Isaiah 7:13-14; 9:2, 6-7; 11:1-10.** Ask:

→ What phrases from the Scripture are familiar because they are part of the Christmas story or used in Christmas hymns?

→ What should we expect from Jesus' birth? What difference did it make to our world and to us?

Close with prayer.

SMALL-GROUP ACTIVITY: LIVING THE STORY (60 minutes)

Supplies needed: Bibles and one print-out each of Group 1, 2, 3, 4, and 5 (on CD-ROM). If you have more than five small groups, print out more copies.

Note: The game should continue from morning to night or from morning to morning, based on how long your retreat is.

Say: "Each small group is going to live out the Christmas story by taking on biblical roles. Your group will be given a sheet explaining your role, but you are not to divulge your group's identity until closing time."

Give each group a handout and Bibles, and send the group off with an adult leader to talk through the questions and decide how to act out its character.

Have a special talk with the recipients of Group 5 handout (the innkeepers). Tell them that traditionally, the innkeeper has had a role in the nativity stories we hear and the plays we see at Christmastime. Scripture doesn't mention the person who turned Mary Joseph away but simply states that there was no room in the inn. You'll have to help Group 5 imagine the person who might have had to tell Joseph and Mary the inn was full.)

LARGE-GROUP ACTIVITY: REVEALING YOUR GROUP'S IDENTITY (90 minutes)

Tell the groups to create a skit that will reveal to everyone the character they have been playing all day long. Give them about thirty minutes to create their skits; then have the groups perform in the order of appearance in the Gospels (Mary, Joseph, angel, and shepherds).

After the skits, ask:

→ How, specifically, did you try to incorporate your characters' traits into your behavior?

→ Was this task difficult, or easy? Why?

→ How did you feel when behaving a certain way to reflect your character?

→ What worked, and what didn't?

→ How well would you rate your group's portrayal of the character you were assigned?

Have some volunteers read **John 1:1-18** aloud. Ask:

→ If you had to explain the Incarnation to someone who had never heard the story in which God became human in Jesus Christ, how would you explain it? Can you think of any metaphors or symbols that would help?

→ What did Jesus "give up" to become human?

→ What aspects of being human are terrific?

→ What aspects of being human can be a real bummer?

→ What might you need to "give up" to follow Christ?

CLOSING EXPERIENCE:
WHO DO YOU SAY THAT I AM?
(15 minutes)

Supplies needed: Choral Reading handouts (on CD-ROM)

Hand out the choral readings, and gather the group in a circle. Designate the "right" and "left" sides, and assign the solo voices. Invite the youth to close your retreat by affirming in a choral reading their belief in Christ.

Lenten Retreat

Focus: to help youth strengthen their faith as they walk through Lent

Key Scripture: "Those who find their life will lose it, and those who lose their life for my sake will find it" (Matthew 10:39).

All of the options below are large-group activities. Arrange the options to fit your schedule. Schedule the Lenten Devotional, Guided Prayer for the Evening, and Stations at the Cross (on CD-ROM) in between the options.

Options
- → Lenten Games
- → Lenten Win, Lose, or Draw
- → Worship: Evidence of the Cross
- → A Personal Journey
- → My Not-to-Do List
- → Holy-Week-Image Identification
- → Servant Scenes
- → My Servant Characteristics
- → Worship: Cross Building
- → Cross Lights: A Closing Worship Experience
- → Nails in the Cross

Reproducible Handouts (on CD-ROM)

- → Lenten Devotional
- → Guided Prayer for the Evening
- → Stations of the Cross

LENTEN GAMES

Lenten Word Scramble
(20 minutes)

Supplies needed: small pieces of paper and differently colored markers

Preparation: Tear the paper into small pieces if you need to. Use a different color of marker to spell each term from the Lenten Word List, writing one letter on each piece of paper. Do as many words as you choose or have time for. Scramble the sheets of paper.

Lenten Word List: *Lent, prayer, cross, Ash Wednesday, Palm Sunday, forty days, Maundy Thursday, Good Friday, ashes, passion, Holy Communion, crucifixion, Holy Week, the upper room, Gethsemane, hosanna*

Give one letter to each person. Ask the youth to find people with the same color of letters, to form a group with those students, and to unscramble the letters to discover the term associated with Lent.

Lenten Quiz
(15 minutes)

Ask the youth the following questions:

1. What is the first day of Lent called? (Ash Wednesday)

2. How long does Lent last? (forty days)

3. What is the day before Lent begins called? (Shrove, or Fat, Tuesday)

4. What is the name of the last week of Lent? (Holy Week)

5. Lent has traditionally been a time for what two spiritual disciplines? (prayer and penitence)

6. What is the liturgical color for this season? (purple)

7. When did Jesus enter Jerusalem riding a donkey? (Palm Sunday)

8. What did the people shout as Jesus rode into Jerusalem? ("Hosanna!")

9. On what day did Jesus institute Holy Communion? (Maundy Thursday)

10. Where did Jesus institute Holy Communion? (the upper room)

11. Where did Jesus pray on the night of his arrest? (the garden of Gethsemane)

12. On what day was Jesus crucified? (Good Friday)

13. What Jewish celebration was happening when Jesus was crucified? (Passover)

14. Where was Jesus crucified? (Golgotha)

15. Where was Jesus buried? (the tomb of Joseph of Arimethea)

Lenten Win, Lose, or Draw
(15 minutes)

Supplies needed: markers, and sixteen index cards, and newsprint or large sheets of paper

Preparation: Copy each word from the Lenten Word List (page 88) on an individual index card.

Divide the group into two or three teams. Give each team markers and sheets of paper.

Next, say: "Taking turns, each team will have a member pick an index card. Then that person will quickly draw for his or her team a picture representing the word or phrase on the card, and his or her team will have to guess it. Numbers, letters, and words are not allowed as clues. Each group will have three minutes to guess and explain to me the word or phrase's significance to the Lenten season. If the group is unable to guess and explain, another team may guess."

Tell each team to choose someone to be the person to pick an index card and draw; then address any questions, and choose the first team to play.

WORSHIP: EVIDENCE OF THE CROSS
(20–30 minutes)

Supplies needed: ashes (available at Christian book stores), Bibles, a CD or cassette tape of worship music (optional), and a CD or cassette player (optional)

Discuss with the youth the symbolism of the ritual for Ash Wednesday, when Christians are marked with a visible sign of the cross. Ask:

→ How can you continue to wear the sign of the cross after the ashes have worn off?

→ Where do you see evidence of the cross in your life? in the lives of others?

Have volunteers read **Ecclesiastes 3:20; 12:7** and **Matthew 10:39.** Ask:

→ Why are ashes an appropriate image for the beginning of Lent?

→ When you think of ways life comes from death, what images come to mind?

→ Can you name persons who found their life by losing it?

→ Have you experienced times when you found your life by losing it?

Invite the students into a time of silent prayer. You might play some worship music or sing some songs together to prepare for the silence. Encourage the youth to examine their hearts and the state of their faith. Invite them to come forward and receive the sign of the cross on their forehead or on their hand when they feel led. When everyone who wants to come forward has done so, pray a prayer of blessing for the students.

A PERSONAL JOURNEY
(10–12 minutes)

Supplies needed: Bibles

Divide your group into three teams, and assign each team one the following Scripture readings: **Matthew 4:1-11; Exodus 24:15-18; 34:27-28; Deuteronomy 8:1-7;** and **Joshua 5:6.** Ask each team to look in its Scripture passage for clues as to why Lent is forty days long.

After a few minutes, ask:

→ What did you find that suggests why Lent is forty days long?

→ Why, do you think, are these stories from the Bible relevant to Lent?

→ What do these stories have to do with Lent as a time of preparation for Easter?

→ What common themes are found in these Scriptures?

MY NOT-TO-DO LIST
(20 minutes)

Supplies needed: a pen or pencil per youth and an index card per youth

Have the youth think of something they need to give up that would create some free time to spend with God and develop the spiritual disciplines of prayer, meditation, journaling, and just resting in God's presence.

Ask:

→ What is the purpose of giving up something for Lent?

→ What impact would giving up something have on your life?

→ How would giving up something draw you closer to God or help you understand Christ's sacrifice on the cross?

→ How would forgoing something on this list as a means of self-denial help deepen your understanding the significance of Christ's sacrifice on the cross?

Hand out the pencils and index cards. Encourage the students to write down some things they might give up or not do during Lent. Challenge the youth to pray about this task and follow through with it. Remind them that the point of forgoing something is to create space and time for God in their lives.

HOLY-WEEK-IMAGE IDENTIFICATION
(20 minutes)

Supplies needed: paper, markers, and thumbtacks or masking tape

Preparation: Post several blank sheets of paper around the meeting area, and put markers near each sheet.

Say: "Around this area are some sheets of paper. Go to one of them, and grab a marker. You and the other youth at each sheet will need to spread out evenly, so that everyone has some room. Write down or draw some images or symbols of Holy Week events."

Ask:

→ Why did you choose your particular image or symbol?

→ What meaning does it have for you?

Say: "Images can provide insight, healing, guidance, and deeper meaning for our experiences. Look at the images, and see if there's one that calls to you, even if it's not the one you wrote or drew. Is there one image that stands out?"

Ask:

→ Which image would you choose to be your focus during Holy Week?

→ Why does this image have special meaning for you? Why do you identify with it?

→ How could this image challenge and guide you?

→ Does the image you've chosen indicate your present emotional state?

SERVANT SCENES
(15 minutes)

Supplies needed: Bibles

Ask four individuals to read the following Scriptures aloud to the group: John 13:3-15; John 15;12-17; Matthew 26:26-28; and Luke 22:24-27.

Divide the youth into small groups, and ask them to discuss the following questions with their group:

→ What servant images show up in these accounts?

→ Why did Jesus model a servant attitude?

→ Why is servanthood an important aspect of Christianity?

→ How does our culture foster or encourage a servant attitude?

→ How does our culture dissuade or belittle a servant attitude?

→ What makes it difficult to choose to be a servant?

MY SERVANT CHARACTERISTICS
(10 minutes)

Say: "I'm about to read off a series of statements. Hold up ten fingers if you think a statement is true for you most of the time, five fingers for sometimes, and one finger for seldom." Read aloud these statements:

→ I consider the needs of others above my own.

→ I try to always think of the good of the group above my desires.

→ I give up my time to help others.

→ I put aside my agenda when a friend needs me.

→ I listen to others more than I talk about myself.

→ I think of ways to be kind and considerate of others.

→ I consider others as of equal importance and value as myself.

→ I can learn a lot from other people and do not need to know all the answers.

→ I would sacrifice to help someone in need.

→ I show compassion to all, both friend and foe.

Ask:

→ When is it particularly difficult to be a servant?

→ Whom do you find it painstaking to serve?

→ How is God challenging you to be a servant?

WORSHIP: CROSS BUILDING
(30-45 minutes)

Supplies needed: magazines, newspapers, paper, pencils, scissors, glue, and a large piece of brown cardboard

Preparation: Cut a large cross out of a piece of cardboard.

Read and identify Christ's last words from the cross in **John 19:25-30** and **Luke 23:33-46.** Say: "Cut out from the newspapers and magazines words and images that reflect the meaning of the cross to you. As a group, glue these cut-outs to the large cross."

After the youth have completed their task, ask:

➔ What do you see when you look at this cross?

➔ Why did you choose those images to put on a cross?

➔ What contrasting images, purposes, and feelings are conveyed in this cross?

CROSS LIGHTS: A CLOSING WORSHIP SERVICE
(20-30 minutes)

Supplies needed: a votive candle for each person, matches, a large mirror, and a table

Place the mirror on a small table so that the mirror is lying flat with the reflective side up. Have the group sit around the table. Give each person one candle. Light your candle, light a youth's candle, and have the students light one another's candles.

Say: "We're going to say together a responsive reading called Cross Lights. After each phrase I say, respond with the phrase *we light a candle of thankfulness.* After the reading, we'll name someone who has been a reflection of the cross for us, and we'll place it on the mirror. As you place your candles, work together to form the shape of the cross with them."

Begin the Cross-Lights Responsive Reading by saying:

➔ For persons who model acceptance, not judgement ...

→ For persons who exhibit an attitude of servanthood ...

→ For persons who offer us refuge and security ...

→ For persons who heal our wounds and hurts ...

→ For persons who forgive us before we ask ...

→ For persons who free us to be ourselves ...

→ For persons who give us unconditional love ...

→ For persons who lead us to the cross ...

Pray: "Thank you, Lord, for the people in our lives who have reflected Christ's love to us. May we be signs of the cross to others. In Jesus' name, Amen."

NAILS IN THE CROSS
(30 minutes)

Supplies needed: a Bible, two pieces of wooden scrap board, a few large nails, a few small nails per youth, a hammer, small slips of paper, and pencils

Preparation: Make a wooden cross out of scrap wood, as big as you want. (The product doesn't have to be pretty, so don't be concerned about your carpentry skills.)

Read aloud **Colossians 2:13-14.**

Provide a piece of paper paper and a pen to each person. Have the youth write one or two words that describe how it feels to be lost, a few words that describe how it feels to be forgiven, and a brief prayer that communicates thanks to God.

Invite each person to nail his or her paper on the cross. When all of the youth have nailed their papers, close with everyone saying together, "Lord, hear our prayers. Amen."